WORTH AT WORK ADVANCE PRAISE

Hospitality has spent years trying to fix burnout, turnover, and inconsistent service with more training, more scripts, and more processes. *Worth at Work* challenges the industry to look deeper, making a compelling case that exceptional service does not come from forcing people to smile harder, but from creating environments where people feel valued, supported, and grounded from the inside out.

What makes this book so impactful is that it speaks directly to what so many hospitality leaders are feeling right now. The industry does not have a people problem. It has an exhaustion problem. Randy Haveson and Kat Nisson offer a much-needed shift in perspective by focusing on the human side of hospitality and reminding us that if we want teams to stay, serve authentically, and truly thrive together, it starts from within.

— **Steve Carran**

Co-Founder, Modern Hotelier Podcast & Media

Worth at Work is a comprehensive, insightful, and easy-to-navigate tool for all professionals striving to achieve and maintain service excellence in their businesses. The concepts of curiosity, engagement, leadership, self-esteem, and teamwork discussed in the book are essential to creating a thriving workplace culture.

As a people and culture professional in the luxury hospitality industry, I believe connecting with others and demonstrating empathy are critical to creating meaningful interactions that exceed expectations. Haveson and Nisson have identified and captured the essence of what is required to consistently deliver exceptional service.

Worth at Work is a must-read.

— **Brenda Tscharner**

People & Culture Hospitality Leadership Consultant

WORTH AT WORK

WORTH AT WORK

AN INSIDE-OUT APPROACH TO CONFIDENT TEAMS AND EXCEPTIONAL SERVICE

RANDY HAVESON, MA
AND
KAT NISSON, MLIS, CPCC

Press 49
4980 South Alma School Road
Suite 2-493
Chandler, Arizona 85248

Published by Press 49, a division of BMH Companies, Chandler, Arizona.

Volume pricing is available for bulk orders from corporations, associations, and others. For bulk order details and media inquiries, please contact Press 49 at info@press49.com or 833.PRESS49 (833.773.7749).

FIRST EDITION

Library of Congress Control Number: 2026909882

ISBN (paperback): 978-1-953315-69-4
ISBN (eBook): 978-1-953315-70-0

BUS107000 BUSINESS & ECONOMICS / Personal Success
BUS081000 BUSINESS & ECONOMICS / Industries / Hospitality, Travel & Tourism
BUS070080 BUSINESS & ECONOMICS / Industries / Service
SEL031000 SELF-HELP / Personal Growth / General

Interior and cover design by Medlar Publishing Solutions Pvt Ltd., India

Printed in the United States of America

TABLE OF CONTENTS

PART THREE

CARING FOR THE WHOLE PERSON

PART FOUR

BUILDING CULTURES WHERE WORTH FLOURISHES

PART FIVE

FROM "I'VE GOT THIS" TO "WE'VE GOT THIS"

ACKNOWLEDGEMENTS

From Randy: There would be no WORTH@WORK without Kat, who has a magical ability to turn my ideas into solid content. She's my translator and my "VP of Everything."

To Eden, who is my inspiration, my heart, and the one who brings the quickest smile to my face.

To Pam, words cannot describe the impact you've had in my life. You ground me, you inspire me, and you help me see things in a different light.

To the dozens of administrators, colleagues, and others who taught me, guided me, and walked with me, thank you. I am who I am today because of what I've learned from all of you.

The most important lesson I've learned is to never forget to play. Let the inner child out every now and then to enjoy the things that life has to offer. We're on an adventure, and I plan to get the most out of it.

From Kat: Randy has spent his life showing people the magic that's already inside them and believing, with his whole heart, that they'll see it too. Thank you for seeing something in me before I saw it myself, and for trusting me to help bring this vision to life.

To Scott, who lets me disappear into the work when I need to, cheers me on through every draft, and always has a hug waiting when I come back up for air. He's the one who talks me off the ledge and makes me laugh before I've even finished climbing down. I love him madly.

To Tad, who teaches me every day what it means to advocate for those who don't yet have a voice. So much of how I led teams came from learning to see the people others might overlook.

To my sister, Rosey, and my parents, who held me up through some very rough years. This work exists because you didn't let me fall.

Randy, I'm Tinkerbell to your Peter Pan, and I've got the faith, the trust, and the pixie dust to prove it. I believe in this book. I believe in you. Now let's fly!

WHY THIS BOOK, WHY NOW

Most people in service industries right now are too exhausted to notice that the systems they're following stopped working a long time ago. They're running plays from a playbook that was already outdated before turnover gutted their teams and the world got harder. They just don't have the bandwidth to step back and see it.

But this isn't new. After every major turning point, the old way of doing things stops working. It happened after the Industrial Revolution. After two World Wars. After the Great Depression. After COVID. Each time, the world changed, and the systems that carried people through the previous era couldn't carry them into the next one. What was needed wasn't a revolution. It was an evolution.

We're in one of those moments right now. The same training doesn't work. The same approach to customer service doesn't work. The reason is simple: People have changed. They want to be seen and heard, on both sides of the front desk.

The organizations they work for keep doubling down on the same approaches, expecting different results. The problem isn't effort. It isn't investment. It's that almost everything the industry has built is designed to shape what people *do* without ever addressing what's happening *inside* the people doing it. And that inner experience, whether someone feels depleted or grounded, invisible or valued, running on fumes or genuinely present, is what determines whether service feels human or mechanical to the person on the receiving end.

This isn't only a hospitality problem, though hospitality is where this book is rooted. The same pattern plays out across industries that serve people: healthcare, senior living, transportation, retail, and customer experience. Anywhere the work asks you to show up for others while quietly running on empty yourself.

Worth at Work was written to name what most organizations have been overlooking and to do something about it. Not by adding more to anyone's plate, but by addressing what's been missing underneath everything else.

When people feel grounded in their own worth, everything else shifts. Interactions become more human. Teams start pulling together instead of just getting through the day. And the kind of service that guests remember and teams are proud of starts happening naturally because the people delivering it actually have something left to give.

That's the shift service industries need right now. It starts from the inside out.

INTRODUCTION: WHEN YOUR STARS ARE BURNING OUT

It's 11:30 on a Friday night, and Maria is at the concierge desk.

The lobby is nearly empty. Somewhere on another floor, a vacuum hums. Through the window, Maria can hear the fountain in the courtyard.

Maria has worked at this property for four years, the last two in VIP services. She's training to be a concierge now, her third overnight shift this week. An hour ago, she sent her husband a few dollars on Venmo for bus fare. He lost his job when the hotel down the coast cut staff, and the new one doesn't start until Monday. Their daughter's science project sits unfinished on the kitchen table. Maria will deal with it tomorrow. Tonight, she just needs to get through her shift.

That's when she sees the woman crossing the lobby.

Maria recognizes her immediately. Her daughter follows her on Instagram. Shows Maria every post. But that's not what catches Maria's attention. It's the way the woman is moving: tight shoulders, jaw set, grip white-knuckled on the deep red Valentino bag at her hip. The gold chain strap has gotten tangled with what appears to be a Cartier brooch. Maria knows the brands because this guest keeps the designer items in their original boxes when she stays here. She takes care of what's loaned to her, unlike some.

The woman reaches the desk to check in. Before Maria can offer a greeting, it spills out: delayed flight, lost luggage, fourteen hours of travel, a press junket tomorrow afternoon, and nothing to wear.

Her voice is controlled but barely.

The standard response is simple: apologize, complete the check-in, and wish her a good stay. Maria has said the words a hundred times.

Instead, she pauses.

"Welcome back," Maria says. "That does sound like a long and exhausting day."

The woman's eyes fill. She looks away slowly, then back. "It's been a long few months."

What comes out over the next few minutes: an international adoption, her third trip to Africa in two months, the uncertainty, the waiting, the paperwork, and the hope that keeps getting tested. The press junket tomorrow, where she'll have to smile and talk about her new project like her whole heart isn't on another continent.

Maria listens and keeps eye contact. She doesn't offer solutions. When there's a pause, she says, "I'm a mom, too. It doesn't matter where you are. Part of you is always with them."

The woman nods. Something in her face shifts.

Maria glances down and notices the brooch, still tangled in the chain.

"You're holding a lot right now." She gestures toward it. "May I?"

The woman looks down, surprised. Maria gently untangles the chain and straightens the brooch.

The woman laughs softly, the tension breaking. "I didn't even notice that it was loose."

"There," Maria says. Then she turns to her screen. "I just upgraded you to a suite on the quiet side of the building. And if you have your baggage claim tag, I'm going to call the airline right now to see if I can expedite your luggage. We'll send you a message the moment it arrives. Do you want a wake-up call, or would you rather sleep as long as you can?"

The woman stares at her for a moment. "Sleep," the woman says softly. Then she pauses, looking at Maria. "Thank you. I … thank you."

She heads toward the elevator. Maria watches the doors close, then picks up the phone to call the airline.

The lobby is quiet again. Her problems haven't gone anywhere. But Maria feels lighter. Less alone than she was ten minutes ago.

That interaction could have gone differently.

Not because Maria isn't skilled. She's exceptional. The property is betting on her future precisely because she's so good at what she does.

But excellence doesn't protect you from depletion. In fact, it often accelerates it. The best people get asked to do more.

They're being moved into facilitating training programs while still covering their regular responsibilities. They become the ones others lean on when staffing gets thin. They hold more, carry more, give more.

And one night, a text about a sick child arrives at the wrong moment, and that sharp internal voice wins, and the celebrity with the loose brooch gets a room instead of a human connection. No complaint. No negative review. Just another forgettable transaction in an industry that's forgotten what makes service memorable.

The hospitality industry is burning through its best people.

Turnover rates in hospitality hover between 70 and 80 percent annually.[1,2] These numbers are so familiar they've become background noise, accepted as simply the cost of doing business in an industry built on human interaction.

But behind those percentages are real people. People like Maria. People who entered this work because they genuinely wanted to take care of others. People who believed hospitality was more than a job. People whose light was bright when they started.

Watch closely, and you'll see the pattern. A new team member arrives with energy, with curiosity, with that spark that makes guests feel welcome. Six months later, the spark dims. A year later, they're going through the motions. Two years later, they're gone. Either physically, having moved on to another property or another industry entirely, or mentally, still showing up but no longer present.

The industry's response has been predictable: more training, better scripts, clearer standards, staff appreciation events,

…tocols, mystery shopper programs, and service recovery.

performance… …ong, exactly. Scripts give people a starting point w… …e new or nervous. Standards create consistency. None … …uilds skills.

… it addresses the real problem.

…t train your way to authentic connection. You …t genuine warmth. You cannot mandate the kind of … makes a guest feel truly seen.

…omes from somewhere else entirely.

From our combined decades of working with people, we've seen that you cannot build confidence by demanding confidence. You cannot create self-esteem by evaluating performance. You cannot inspire genuine hospitality by telling people to smile harder.

Authentic service comes from authentic worth. When people feel genuinely worthy, not because of what they produce or how they perform, but as a baseline condition of being human, they show up differently. Their warmth isn't manufactured. Their attention isn't forced. Their ability to connect with a struggling guest at 11:30 p.m. comes naturally because they're operating from a place of fullness rather than depletion.

This book is about building that foundation.

It's about understanding what's actually happening inside your team members when they interact with guests and what makes the difference between competent service and memorable service.

It's about the critical internal voice that r… ost people's heads and how to help them develop a kinde… t serves them better.

Energy matters here, too: what fills it, what … how to protect it in an industry that demands const…

We'll look at the four dimensions of a whole perso… cal, mental, emotional, spiritual) and why neglecting any … them eventually undermines everything else.

Psychological safety gets its own focus, including why "… customer is always right" might be the most damaging phrase i… hospitality leadership.

And finally, this book is about what happens when individual growth meets collective purpose, when a group of people who've each done their own inner work comes together with a shared commitment to something larger than themselves.

We call that "We Over Me." And it changes everything.

The approach in this book won't fix broken systems overnight. It won't eliminate difficult guests, impossible situations, or the genuine challenges of running a hospitality operation.

What it will do is give you a different foundation to build on. And here's something we want you to know before we go any further: You don't have to do all of this at once. This book lays out a full picture of what's possible, but even a few small changes will move you somewhere better than where you are right now. If you're tired, if you've been at this for years and feel like you've already done everything you can think of; if you cannot imagine taking on one more thing, start with whatever feels doable. We're here to help you find the pieces that fit.

Instead of training people on what to do and hoping they feel good enough to do it well, you'll learn to build their sense of worth first, and watch the "what to do" flow naturally from that foundation.

Instead of treating turnover as inevitable, you'll understand what's actually driving your best people away and how to create environments where they want to stay.

Instead of teams that function as collections of individuals, you'll build genuine cohesion. Groups of people who trust each other, support each other, and share a belief that "we've got this" even when things get hard.

The hospitality industry is facing a choice. Keep doing what we've been doing (more scripts, more standards, more training programs that address symptoms while ignoring root causes) and accept the results you've been getting.

Or do something different.

Build people from the inside out. Create environments where worth is the foundation. Develop leaders who inspire rather than intimidate. Foster teams that operate from "We Over Me."

That's the invitation of this book.

Your stars don't have to burn out. Let's talk about how to help them shine.

PART ONE

THE PROBLEM BENEATH THE PROBLEM

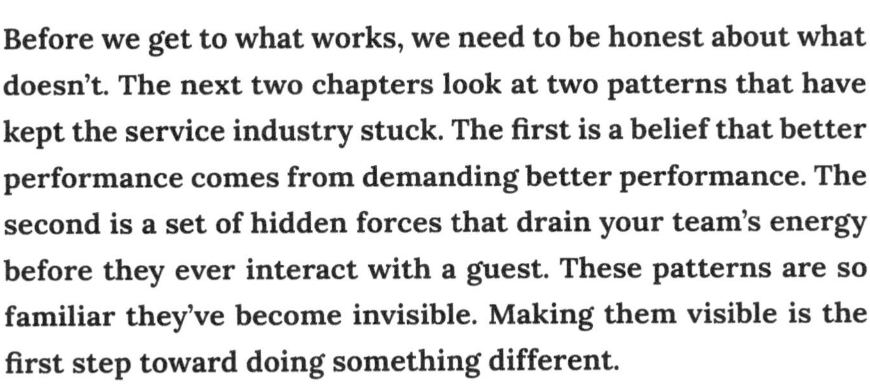

Before we get to what works, we need to be honest about what doesn't. The next two chapters look at two patterns that have kept the service industry stuck. The first is a belief that better performance comes from demanding better performance. The second is a set of hidden forces that drain your team's energy before they ever interact with a guest. These patterns are so familiar they've become invisible. Making them visible is the first step toward doing something different.

CHAPTER 1

THE SMILE HARDER TRAP

You've heard it before. Maybe you've said it yourself.

"Just smile. Be friendly. Follow the script."

It sounds reasonable. Smiling is free. Friendliness costs nothing. Scripts ensure consistency. And when you're managing a team of people across multiple shifts, dealing with staffing shortages, and demanding guests and razor-thin margins, "smile harder" feels like a solution you can actually implement.

The problem is that it doesn't work.

Not in the way that matters. Not in the way that creates the kind of service guests remember, talk about, and return for. Not in the way that keeps your best people from burning out and walking away.

The "smile harder" approach treats service like a performance. Hit your marks. Say your lines. Project warmth, whether you feel it or not. And when guest satisfaction scores dip or a complaint comes in, the solution is always the same: more training on what to say, more reminders to be friendly, more pressure to perform.

In working with hospitality teams, we've noticed a pattern: *The problem is rarely that people don't know what to do. It's that something is happening inside them that makes authentic connection impossible.*

You cannot perform your way to genuine warmth. And guests know the difference.

THE PERFECTLY FORGETTABLE EXPERIENCE

Think about the last time you checked into a hotel after a long day of travel.

The person at the front desk probably smiled. They probably said something like, "Welcome to [Hotel Name]. How was your trip?" They probably processed your check-in efficiently, handed you your key cards, and pointed toward the elevators.

Nothing went wrong. The interaction was fine.

But what do you actually remember about it? Probably nothing. Because "fine" doesn't create memories. "Fine" doesn't build loyalty. "Fine" is what happens when someone follows the script without being fully present for the human being standing in front of them.

Now think about a service interaction you actually remember. One where you walked away feeling genuinely cared for. What made it different?

Chances are, it wasn't the script. It was the person. Something about them was fully there. They noticed something specific about you. They responded to what you actually needed, not just what you asked for. They made you feel like a person, not a transaction.

That's the gap the hospitality industry keeps trying to close through training programs, service standards, and mystery shopper evaluations. And it keeps not working. Because you cannot train presence. You cannot mandate authenticity. You cannot script the thing that makes service memorable.

THE REAL COST OF MECHANICAL SERVICE

The consequences of a "smile harder" culture manifest in two areas: guest experience and employee retention.

On the guest side, mechanical service creates a ceiling. Your property will never be terrible (assuming basic competence), but it will also never be remarkable. You'll hover in the middle of review sites, generating feedback like "clean rooms, friendly staff, nothing special." Guests will have no reason to choose you over a competitor. Price becomes the only differentiator.

But the greater cost is what happens to your people.

When you ask human beings to perform warmth they don't feel, something breaks down over time. Sociologist Arlie Hochschild calls it "emotional labor," the work of managing your emotions to fulfill the requirements of a job. In small doses, everyone does this.[1] But when emotional labor becomes the primary demand of your role, when you're expected to smile through exhaustion, project calm through chaos, and radiate warmth while running on empty, the toll accumulates.

This is why your best people burn out. Not because they lack resilience or commitment, but because they're doing invisible work that never gets acknowledged or supported. They're performing a version of themselves for eight, ten, or twelve hours a day, and nobody is helping them refill the tank.

The industry calls this turnover. We call it a failure of imagination.

WHAT SCRIPTS ACTUALLY DO (AND WHAT THEY DON'T)

Let's be clear: We're not against scripts. Scripts serve important functions, especially for new team members who are still learning the rhythm of service interactions. A good script provides scaffolding. It gives people language to use when they're nervous or uncertain. It creates consistency across a team.

But not all scripts are created equal.

Some sound like they were written by someone who's never had a real conversation.

"Welcome to [Property Name]. My name is [Your Name]. How may I assist you today?" Fill in the blanks, say the words, move on. These scripts prioritize uniformity over connection. They treat team members as robots to be programmed.

Others leave room for the human delivering them. "Make the guest feel genuinely welcomed. Use their name if you have it. Notice something real about their experience." These scripts guide without constraining. They trust the person holding them.

The problem arises when scripts become the ceiling rather than the floor.

When leaders treat the script as the goal, rather than the starting point, something important gets lost. Team members learn that compliance is what matters. They stop paying attention to the actual human in front of them because they're focused on hitting their marks. The script becomes a shield against genuine engagement rather than a foundation for it.

We've seen companies where team members were so focused on saying the "right" words that they missed obvious cues from guests. The script said to ask "How was your trip?" so they asked it, even when the guest was visibly upset, or rushing, or clearly not in the mood for small talk. The words were right. The guest still felt unseen.

The best service happens when someone knows the script well enough to adapt it. It happens when they understand the intent behind the words and feel confident enough to respond to what's actually happening in the moment. That kind of flexibility doesn't come from more training on what to say. It comes from something deeper.

When service falls flat, the typical response is to examine what people are doing wrong. Are they following the script? Are they smiling enough? Are they using the guest's name? The focus stays external, on behaviors that can be observed, measured, and corrected.

But what if the problem isn't what your people are doing? What if the problem is what's happening inside them while they're doing it?

Consider two team members handling the same situation: a guest who arrives frustrated after a delayed flight, a lost bag, and a rental car that wasn't ready. Both team members follow the same script. Both apologize for the inconvenience. Both offer the same service recovery options.

But one interaction leaves the guest feeling handled, and the other leaves them feeling seen. One team member was going through the motions, and the other was genuinely present. The guest may not be able to articulate what was different, but they felt it.

The difference wasn't training. It wasn't the script. It wasn't even necessarily experience.

The difference was what was happening inside each team member. One was operating from depletion, self-protection, and a desire to just get through the interaction. The other was operating from a sense of inner stability, from a place that allowed them to actually see the frustrated human being in front of them and respond with authentic warmth.

That inner difference is what this book is about.

BEYOND "SMILE HARDER"

The hospitality industry has spent decades perfecting the external elements of service: polished scripts, clear standards, and comprehensive training programs.

What's been missing is attention to the internal experience of the people delivering that service. What's happening in their minds when they greet a guest? What voice is running in their heads when something goes wrong? How full or depleted is their emotional tank? Do they feel supported, or are they just hoping to survive until the end of their shift?

These questions don't show up on performance evaluations. Mystery shoppers do not measure them. But they determine everything about the quality of service your guests actually receive.

The "smile harder" trap is believing that if you just get the external elements right, the internal experience will follow. If people act warmly, they'll start to feel warm. That performance creates reality.

It actually works the other way around.

When people feel genuinely worthy, not because of their performance, but as a baseline condition of being human, authentic warmth becomes natural. When they're not spending energy managing their internal critic, they have more attention available for the person in front of them. When they work in environments that support their whole selves, they don't burn out performing a version of themselves for eight hours straight.

This is what we mean by building people from the inside out. It's not about abandoning scripts, standards, or training. It's about recognizing that none of those things work the way you want unless you first attend to what's happening inside the people expected to deliver.

In the chapters that follow, we'll explore what it actually looks like to build service culture from the inside out.

We'll introduce the concept of the "energy ball" and help you understand what fills and drains your team member's capacity for genuine connection. We'll examine the internal voice that runs in most people's heads (what Randy calls the "bully voice") and show you how to help people develop a kinder alternative (the "best friend voice"). We'll walk through the four dimensions of a whole person (physical, mental, emotional, and spiritual) and explain why neglecting any one of them eventually undermines everything else.

We'll talk about what leaders need to do differently. We'll cover what leaders need to do differently, psychological safety and why it matters more than almost any other factor in service quality, and the shift from "me" to "we" that transforms a collection of individuals into a genuine team.

We'll give you practical tools you can actually use. Not more scripts, but frameworks for understanding what's happening inside your people and how to support them.

The smile harder trap is seductive because it's simple. It asks nothing of leaders except to demand more from their teams. But it doesn't work, and the evidence is everywhere: in turnover numbers, mediocre reviews, and the exhausted faces of people who entered this industry because they wanted to take care of others and are now just hoping to make it to the end of their shift.

There's another way. Let's explore it together.

Randy Remembers: The Two Bellmen

Two bellmen. Same shift. Same union rotation. Same random assignment of guests.

During his time as a greeter at a resort, Randy watched them both. Every morning, he'd ask the same question: "Hey, how's your day going?"

The first bellman: "Rough day. Guests have been demanding, tips are low, nothing's going right."

The second bellman: "What a great day! I've had the best guests. Best tips I've had in months!"

Same guests. Same job. Completely different experiences.

The guests could tell the difference instantly. That's what fascinated him. Not because of anything the bellmen said or did "wrong." The service was technically correct in both cases. They followed the same scripts and hit the same marks. But one interaction felt like a transaction. The other felt like a gift.

CHAPTER 2

THE ENERGY VAMPIRES AMONG US

Every hospitality professional knows the feeling.

You clock in feeling reasonably okay. Maybe you are not fully rested and are definitely carrying some stress from home, but you are functional and ready to work. Then things start to unravel. A guest interaction goes sideways. A coworker dumps their frustration on you. A manager makes a comment that stings. The system crashes during a rush. A family member texts with a crisis you have no power to solve from behind a desk.

By hour four, you feel like a different person. The patience you started with has evaporated. The smile takes effort now. You're not giving less because you care less. You're giving less because something has been taken from you, and nothing has refilled it.

This is not a character flaw. This is not a lack of professionalism. This is how energy works.

Until we understand it, we'll keep losing our best people to a drain that's completely invisible on any performance metric.

Energy vampires come in three forms: the people, the circumstances, and the systems that drain your team's reserves. Some of them work alongside you. Some of them never set foot in your building. Some of them are the building itself.

THE ENERGY BALL

Randy developed a way of visualizing this, first introduced in *Becoming Your Own BFF*, that we've found useful with teams across hospitality settings.[1] We'll explore the energy ball in much greater depth in chapter 5.

Imagine your capacity for genuine engagement, your ability to be fully present and warmly connected with another person, as a ball. When you're fully resourced (well-rested, emotionally stable, supported by your environment), that ball is large. Think beach ball. You have plenty to give. Interactions don't deplete you because you're operating from abundance.

But that ball isn't static. It expands and contracts in response to what's happening to you, around you, and inside you. Every demand on your energy shrinks it a little. Every source of replenishment grows it back.

When the ball is beach-ball-sized, you barely notice the small withdrawals. A mildly irritating guest? No problem. A coworker who forgot to restock something? You handle it. The energy cost is real but manageable.

When the ball shrinks to tennis-ball size, those same interactions start to sting. You feel the withdrawal. You have to actively manage your responses because your natural reserves are running low.

When the ball hits marble size, you're in survival mode. There's nothing left to give. Every interaction costs more than you have. The smile becomes a performance. The warmth disappears. You're physically present and emotionally gone.

Most of the time, leaders cannot tell from the outside how big someone's energy ball is. The same team member might handle an identical situation beautifully on Tuesday and poorly on Friday. The situation didn't change. Their internal resources did.

WHAT DRAINS THE BALL

Energy drains come from everywhere. Some are obvious; others are invisible. We find it helpful to think about them in categories.

Guests and Families

Hospitality work means constant contact with people who are often stressed, tired, or in vacation mode. Travel is exhausting. Being away from home is disorienting. Your team absorbs this all day, every day.

Most guests aren't intentionally difficult. They're just humans having their own experience. But absorbing someone else's stress, frustration, or sadness takes something out of you, even when you handle it perfectly. Multiply that by dozens of interactions per shift, week after week, and the cumulative drain is substantial.

Then there are the genuinely difficult interactions. The guest who speaks to your team member as if they're less than human. The family member who makes inappropriate demands. The person whose entitlement seems bottomless. These interactions don't just drain energy. They can feel like an assault on someone's sense of worth.

The Workplace Itself

Sometimes the biggest energy vampires work at your property.

The manager who leads through criticism and rarely acknowledges what's going well. The veteran team member who has decided nothing will ever change and makes sure everyone knows it. The colleague who treats every shift like a competition and undermines others to look better. The broken systems that make simple tasks frustrating. The chronic understaffing that means everyone is always stretched too thin.

These drains are particularly damaging because they're constant. A difficult guest eventually leaves. A toxic work environment is there every single shift.

Life Outside Work

Your team members have lives beyond your property. They have partners who lose jobs and send Venmo requests for bus fare.

They have children with science projects and aging parents who need care. They have health concerns, financial stress, relationship struggles, and all the ordinary chaos of being human.

When someone clocks in, it's difficult to leave those concerns in their car. They carry them. Those concerns take up space in the energy ball, leaving less energy available for the work itself.

None of this is an excuse for poor performance. But it's an explanation that matters if you want to actually solve the problem rather than just manage the symptoms.

WHY YOUR BEST PEOPLE ARE THE BIGGEST TARGETS

The people most likely to burn out are often your highest performers.

There are a few reasons for this.

They care more. The team member who genuinely wants guests to feel welcomed expends more energy than the one who's just going through the motions. Authentic engagement is more demanding than mechanical service. Every time your best people create a real connection with a guest, they're giving something of themselves. That giving is what makes them excellent. It's also what depletes them faster.

They're asked to do more. When you have a team member who handles difficult situations well, you send them the difficult situations. When someone is reliable, they get more responsibility. When someone excels, they get moved into training programs while still covering their regular duties. Excellence gets rewarded with additional demands while operating on the same finite energy supply.

They often have trouble setting boundaries. The same disposition that makes someone great at service (empathy, responsiveness, a desire to help) makes it hard for them to say no. They cover extra shifts. They stay late. They take on problems that aren't theirs. They absorb stress that others deflect.

They feel failures more deeply. When something goes wrong, your highest performers don't shrug it off. They replay it. They wonder what they could have done differently. That internal processing is part of what makes them good, but it also drains energy that others don't spend.

The result is a cruel irony: The people you most need to retain are the ones most likely to burn out. And because they're often skilled at hiding their depletion, you may not notice until they hand in their resignation or show up one day completely checked out.

THE SLOW DIM

Burnout rarely happens all at once. It's usually a gradual process, what we call the "slow dim."

In the early stages, people compensate. They're tired, but they push through. They feel the drain, but they tell themselves it's temporary. They might not even recognize what's happening because the changes are incremental.

Then the compensation strategies start to fail. The caffeine stops working as well. The weekend doesn't feel like enough recovery time. The things that used to replenish (hobbies, friendships, exercise) get dropped because there's no energy left for them. The person becomes more isolated and more depleted, with fewer resources to draw on.

Eventually, the light goes out. Not dramatically, usually. Just a quiet shift from someone who was fully present to someone who's going through the motions. They're still showing up, following the script, and technically doing their job. But the thing that made them special is gone.

Sometimes they leave at this point. Often, they stay, becoming part of the environment that drains others. The cycle continues.

SPOTTING THE DRAIN BEFORE IT'S TOO LATE

If you're leading a team, learning to recognize early signs of energy depletion is one of the most valuable skills you can develop. What to watch for:

Behavioral changes: Someone who used to volunteer for extra tasks stops offering. Someone who was socially engaged with colleagues becomes withdrawn. Someone who handled difficult situations with grace starts snapping or seems irritated. Watch for the change, the difference from their baseline, not the behavior itself.

Physical signs: These are seen in the fatigue that doesn't seem to resolve with rest, more frequent illness, changes in appearance that suggest self-care is slipping, or moving more slowly than usual.

Emotional shifts: You detect a cynicism that wasn't there before. You hear complaints about things they used to take in stride and expressions of hopelessness about the job, the team, or the industry. There's tearfulness or emotional volatility that seems out of character.

Performance patterns: Inconsistency replaces reliability. Mistakes are showing up from someone who was previously meticulous. They are calling in sick more frequently and arriving late when they used to be early.

None of these signs alone means someone is burning out. Patterns matter. If you're paying attention, you'll notice when someone's energy ball is shrinking before they hit marble size.

The challenge is that noticing isn't enough. You also need to do something about it. We'll talk about what that looks like in later chapters, but the starting point is simply this: Begin treating energy as a real resource that needs to be monitored and managed, not an infinite supply that people are expected to provide regardless of circumstances.

ENERGY IS CONTAGIOUS

Here's one more thing about energy that matters for teams: It spreads.

When you walk into a room where everyone is depleted, frustrated, and running on empty, you'll feel it before anyone says a word. The heaviness is palpable. Now walk into a room where people are genuinely energized, connected, and enjoying their work. It's a different feeling entirely.

This contagion works in both directions.

A single chronically negative team member can drag down everyone around them. These are the energy vampires the chapter title named, and they're not always the people you'd expect. They can be colleagues, guests, systems, or the conditions you work inside every day. Their complaints become the background noise. Their cynicism seeps into conversations. Their depleted energy pulls from others' reserves.

But a single genuinely positive presence lifts the room, too. Not forced positivity (that's exhausting in its own way), but authentic energy that comes from someone who's resourced and present. That kind of energy is generative. It gives to others rather than taking from them.

The collective environment either supports or undermines everyone's ability to show up fully. That's what makes protecting your team's energy a shared responsibility, not just an individual one. When you let energy vampires, whether people, systems, or practices, operate unchecked, you're not just hurting their direct targets. You're degrading the whole team.

Who's responsible for managing energy? The individual team member? The leader? The organization?

The honest answer is all of them.

Individuals have some control over their energy. The choices they make outside of work (sleep, nutrition, relationships, how they spend their recovery time) affect what they bring to each shift. Their internal dialogue, the way they process difficult interactions, their ability to set boundaries. These all matter.

But individuals operate within systems. Those systems either support energy management or actively undermine it.

A team member has limited power to protect their energy when they're chronically understaffed, when their manager leads through fear, when they're expected to absorb abusive guest behavior without support, or when they work unpredictable schedules that prevent real recovery.

This book will address both sides. We'll give individuals tools to understand and protect their own energy. We'll also challenge leaders and organizations to examine how their practices either drain or replenish the people they depend on.

You want your team to show up like Maria at midnight, fully present, genuinely warm, able to see a struggling guest as a human being rather than a problem to solve. That kind of service is only possible when people have energy to give. Right now, most hospitality environments are designed in ways that systematically deplete that energy without intentionally replenishing it.

That's what we're here to change.

PART TWO

BUILDING FROM THE INSIDE OUT

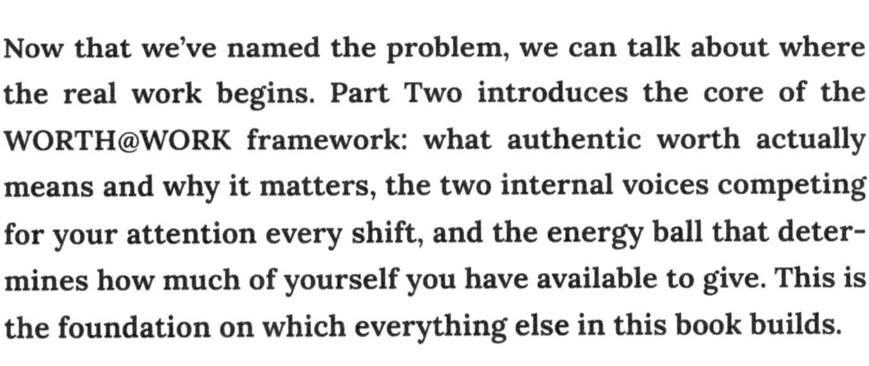

Now that we've named the problem, we can talk about where the real work begins. Part Two introduces the core of the WORTH@WORK framework: what authentic worth actually means and why it matters, the two internal voices competing for your attention every shift, and the energy ball that determines how much of yourself you have available to give. This is the foundation on which everything else in this book builds.

CHAPTER 3

THE WORTH REVOLUTION

Most of us learned a lie so early and so thoroughly that we no longer even recognize it as a lie.

The lie goes something like this: If you perform well enough, achieve enough, get enough external validation, you'll eventually feel confident and worthy. Success creates self-esteem. Accomplishment builds confidence. Do the right things, hit the right markers, and the good feelings will follow.

It sounds logical. It's how most of us were raised. It's certainly how most workplaces operate, with performance reviews, metrics, and recognition programs all built on the assumption that external validation creates internal stability.

It doesn't work that way. The evidence is everywhere.

Think about the highest achievers you know. Are they the most confident, most secure, most internally stable people in your life? Or are many of them driven by anxiety, never quite satisfied, always chasing the next accomplishment that will finally make them feel enough?

Think about your own experience. Have your achievements ever permanently resolved your self-doubt? Or does the relief fade quickly, replaced by new worries about maintaining what you've achieved or reaching the next level?

The lie persists because it contains a grain of truth: Accomplishment does feel good. Recognition does provide a temporary boost. But that boost is exactly that: temporary. It doesn't build lasting confidence because the equation is backward.

Authentic worth doesn't come from performance. It's the other way around. Build worth first, and performance follows. Inside out, not outside in.

The people who show up with genuine confidence and warmth aren't always operating with a goal of recognition and acknowledgment. Randy has learned this through decades of working with people in recovery, in personal development, and now in hospitality. They're operating from a baseline sense of their own worth that exists independent of their performance.

This is a fundamental shift in how we think about supporting people.

The traditional approach says: Teach people what to do, evaluate their performance, reward success, and correct failure, and they'll gradually build confidence through positive results.

The inside-out approach says: Help people recognize their inherent worth first, build their internal stability, and watch their performance naturally improve because they're no longer spending energy managing self-doubt.

Both approaches can produce competent employees. But only one produces the kind of service that guests actually remember. That's because guests don't just experience what you do. They experience who you're being while you do it. And who you're being is determined by what's happening inside you.

When someone operates from a place of authentic worth, their attention is available for the person in front of them. They're not managing an internal critic. They're not performing confidence they don't feel. They're not protecting themselves from the possibility of failure. They're simply present, which is the foundation of genuine connection.

When someone operates from self-doubt, a significant portion of their mental energy goes to managing that doubt. They're watching themselves, evaluating their performance in real time, worrying about how they're coming across. That internal management is exhausting and distracting. It creates exactly the kind of self-conscious service that guests experience as hollow or mechanical.

Randy learned this firsthand. He never once thought, "Here comes another one." Every guest was an individual, a new moment. That simple shift changed everything about how guests responded to him.

THE EGO VS. SELF-ESTEEM CONTINUUM

One of Randy's core frameworks helps clarify what we mean by "authentic worth" versus the kind of confidence that's actually just ego in disguise.

Imagine a continuum. On one end is ego. On the other end is genuine self-esteem.

These two things can look similar from the outside. Both produce confident behavior. Both allow people to take risks, assert themselves, and handle challenging situations. But they come from completely different places and produce completely different results under pressure.

Ego-driven confidence is built on external validation and can come across as cocky. It requires constant feeding. It depends on comparison (being better than others) and on outcomes (succeeding at what you attempt). When the external validation stops, when you fail, or when someone outperforms you, the confidence collapses. Ego is fragile precisely because it's built on things outside your control.

Ego-driven people in service roles often look impressive. They may be charming, polished, and skilled at creating good impressions. But watch what happens when something goes wrong, a guest criticizes them, they make a visible mistake, or a colleague outshines them. The mask slips, and defensiveness emerges. Suddenly, the situation becomes about them and their need to restore their image, not about the guest or co-worker who needs help.

Self-esteem-driven confidence is built on an internal foundation. External validation is still nice, but it's not required for confidence to exist. It doesn't collapse when you fail because your worth isn't contingent on success. It allows you to acknowledge mistakes, receive feedback, and encounter criticism without experiencing them as threats to your identity.

Self-esteem-driven people in service roles might seem less flashy than their ego-driven counterparts. They're not performing confidence. They simply *are* confident. They're simply stable. That stability allows them to stay focused on the guest even when things go sideways. A complaint doesn't trigger defensiveness because it's not experienced as an attack on their worth. A mistake is just a mistake, something to fix and learn from, not evidence of inadequacy.

The goal isn't to eliminate ego. We all have ego, and it serves some useful functions. *The goal is to build a foundation of genuine self-esteem strong enough that ego doesn't run the show.*

WHAT THIS LOOKS LIKE IN PRACTICE

Let's make this concrete: same situation, two different internal foundations.

A guest approaches the front desk, clearly agitated. "I've been waiting twenty minutes for someone to bring up extra towels. I called twice. This is ridiculous for what you charge per night."

The ego-driven response (internal): *This isn't my fault. Housekeeping dropped the ball. Why is this person attacking me? I need to make sure they know I didn't do anything wrong. I'm good at my job. This reflects badly on me, even though I had nothing to do with it.*

The ego-driven response (external): "*I'm so sorry about that. Let me check on what happened.*" (Said with a slight edge, a subtle defensiveness. The team member may also throw housekeeping under the bus, implicitly or explicitly, to protect their own image.)

The self-esteem-driven response (internal): *This person is frustrated. Twenty minutes is a long time to wait for something simple. This isn't about me. How do I fix this for them?*

The self-esteem-driven response (external): "*I'm sorry that happened. You're right, twenty minutes is way too long. Let me get those towels to you right now, and I'll follow up to make sure this doesn't happen again during your stay.*" (Said with genuine acknowledgment, no defensiveness, attention fully on the guest's experience.) And said while picking up the phone to call housekeeping to relay the urgency of the request.

Same script, almost. But the guest feels the difference. In the first interaction, they sense they've been managed. In the second, they feel heard.

This difference multiplies across hundreds of interactions per day, across every team member, across every shift. The cumulative effect is either a property where guests feel genuinely cared for or one where service is competent but forgettable.

Kat's Story: The COVID Meeting Room Crisis

Leading a team of eighty frontline employees during the height of COVID was like conducting an orchestra where half the sheet music kept changing mid-performance. We had protocols. Lots of protocols. One afternoon, those protocols collided with a longtime guest who just wanted things "the way they'd always been."

I was in my office when I heard the commotion. Actually, "heard" is generous. I felt it. That particular frequency of frustration that makes your shoulders tense before your brain even registers what's happening.

The gentleman, dressed to the nines in his bespoke suit at the front desk, was animated; my team member was frozen, and I could see other guests starting to look up from their phones.

Here's what happened in my body before my brain could catch up: My chest tightened, stomach dropped, and my first thought wasn't "How can I help this guest?" or even "How can I support my team member?"

It was: "Please don't make a scene in my lobby."

Pure ego. I was worried about how this looked, how it reflected on me, and whether higher-ups would hear about it. My internal critic was already writing the incident report in my head, casting me as the director of operations who had lost control.

But then I caught myself. I took one breath and shifted. My team member's face told me everything I needed to know. They weren't incompetent or uncaring. They were trapped between a VIP guest's reasonable expectations and an inflexible protocol, standing there like a referee in a game where the rules kept changing.

I walked over, and instead of swooping in with "Let me handle this" energy, I said to my team member, "Walk me through what's happening." Not to catch them in a mistake, but because I genuinely didn't know what options we'd already explored.

Turns out, the guest had secured our largest meeting room for the week, same as he had done on his previous visits.

He'd carefully selected it because social distancing was easy in that space. But our new protocols said different cleaning schedules, limited access hours, and capacity restrictions. Both positions made perfect sense. Both were also completely stuck.

So instead of defending the rules or overriding them dramatically, I asked the guest, "What matters most to you about having this space?" He needed a quiet place to work between his larger in-room meetings and smaller appointments, and he wanted to leave his materials set up. We found a workaround that honored safety protocols and his actual need.

The real work, though, came next. That evening, I realized if this guest was confused, my entire team of eighty was operating without a net. We'd given them rules but not frameworks. Scripts, but not understanding.

I scheduled well-timed huddles over the next week. Not to lecture, but to ask: "What situations are you running into that our protocols don't cover? Where are you getting stuck?" And then (this was the important part), I listened.

We adjusted protocols where we could. Where we couldn't, I at least armed the team with the why behind the rules and some language to help guests understand. More importantly, I got executive leadership buy-in to communicate these more flexible approaches to the entire team. Having leadership visibly support this shift gave my team confidence that they wouldn't be penalized for using good judgment. Without that endorsement, they would have been far less confident moving forward.

Looking back, the difference between my first reaction and my actual response was everything. Ego wanted to protect my image. Self-esteem trusted that I could handle a messy moment and help my team learn to do the same. Ego made it about me. Self-esteem made it about all of us figuring it out together.

Let's be honest: There are times we all wish we had an office door to hide behind. But that afternoon taught me that the best leadership happens when you walk toward the uncomfortable moments instead of away from them.

THE NEUROSCIENCE OF FEAR VS. WORTH

This isn't just philosophy. There's brain science behind why internal state matters so much for service quality.

When we feel threatened (and self-doubt is a form of internal threat), our nervous system shifts into a protective mode. Neuroscience research shows that the prefrontal cortex, responsible for complex thinking, creativity, and empathy, becomes less accessible under stress.[1] Our attention narrows. We become more reactive and less responsive. We lose access to exactly the capacities we most need for genuine human connection.

When we feel safe and stable internally, the opposite happens. The prefrontal cortex stays online. We maintain access to empathy, creativity, and flexible thinking. We can take in new information, read social cues accurately, and respond to what's actually happening rather than reacting from a defensive posture.

This is why "just be more confident" doesn't work as advice. If someone's nervous system is in threat mode, telling them to be confident is like telling someone who's drowning to just swim better. The problem isn't that they don't know how to swim. The problem is they're drowning.

Building authentic worth changes the internal environment. It reduces the baseline threat level. It creates conditions where confidence emerges naturally rather than having to be performed through an internal state of alarm.

WORTH IS NOT EARNED

One of the hardest shifts to make, for individuals and organizations alike, is recognizing that worth is not something you earn. Your connection to it can be strengthened with awareness, practice, and support.

This runs counter to almost everything we've been taught. We live in a culture that constantly evaluates, ranks, and assigns value based on performance. From grades in school to performance reviews at work, we're trained to believe that our value is contingent on what we produce.

But contingent value creates contingent confidence. If my worth depends on my performance, then every performance is a test of my worth. Every interaction carries stakes beyond the interaction itself. I'm not just helping this guest. I'm attempting to prove I'm valuable.

That's exhausting. It shows up in the quality of service.

Inherent worth doesn't mean everyone performs equally well. It doesn't mean standards don't matter or that feedback isn't important. It means that your fundamental value as a human being isn't determined by how well you perform on any given day. You have value simply because you exist.

When people truly grasp this (not just as an idea, but in their bones), something shifts. The stakes of each interaction drop. Performance actually improves because people aren't spending energy defending their worth. They're just doing their job, present and engaged, without the extra weight of existential evaluation.

BUILDING WORTH IN OTHERS

Leaders sometimes ask how they can help their team members build authentic worth. The honest answer: You can't give someone a sense of their own worth. That's internal work they have to do. But you can create conditions that either support or undermine that work.

You undermine worth when you:

- Treat people as interchangeable parts rather than individuals.
- Withhold praise and focus only on correction.
- Make approval contingent on perfection.
- Respond to mistakes with shame rather than learning.
- Allow guests or colleagues to treat team members as less than human.
- Create competition that makes people feel they have to tear others down to rise.

You support worth when you:

- See and acknowledge people as whole human beings, not just their job function.
- Recognize effort and growth, not just outcomes.
- Respond to mistakes as opportunities for learning rather than evidence of inadequacy.
- Protect your team from abusive treatment by guests or colleagues.
- Create an environment where people feel safe being imperfect.

Most of all, do this work yourself. They watch how you handle difficult situations, respond to chaos, and acknowledge success or learning opportunities. Leading by example is the best way to create lasting change.

None of this means lowering standards. In fact, research by Harvard's Amy Edmondson suggests that psychological safety and high standards go together.[2] People perform better when they're not spending energy protecting their sense of worth. But you have to build the safety first. Standards without safety produce anxiety, defensiveness, and, ultimately, the kind of mechanical service we described in chapter 1.

We call this a "worth revolution" because it requires a fundamental shift in how we think about service excellence.

The old model: Hire for skill, train for behavior, evaluate for performance, reward success, and punish failure. People are resources to be optimized.

The new model: Hire for disposition, build worth first, train for skill on a foundation of internal stability, and create environments where authentic connection can flourish. People are whole humans whose internal experiences directly shape the external service they provide.

This shift isn't soft or naive. It's practical. The organizations that figure this out will have lower turnover, higher guest satisfaction, and team members who actually want to come to work. The ones that keep struggling to optimize the old model will keep getting the same mediocre results, no matter how polished their scripts become.

The revolution starts with a simple recognition: You cannot smile your way to genuine warmth. You cannot perform your way to authentic presence. You cannot script the thing that makes service memorable.

You have to build it from the inside out.

Randy's Story: Why Did I Even Apply?

When I was hired at my first university position, I was terrified. I remember thinking, "Why did I even apply? I don't know how to do this. I was expelled from college twice. And now I'm going to work at one?!"

I was insecure, scared, and full of self-doubt. I handled it the way many people do: I overcompensated. I acted like I knew more than I did. I made everything about proving myself, protecting my image, and making sure no one discovered I didn't belong there. The voice in my head was relentless. Every mistake confirmed what I already believed: I wasn't enough.

My supervisor saw what was happening. She'd call me into her office, not to criticize, but to coach. She knew it was my first job in the field, and she kept redirecting me back to what actually mattered.

About four or five months in, something shifted. I realized I wasn't there to prove anything to anyone. I wasn't there to impress the administrators or protect my reputation. I was there for the students. I was there to help them navigate their own journeys, figure out who they were, and where they fit.

Once I stopped making it about me, my confidence actually grew. Not the fragile kind that needs constant validation. The kind that comes from knowing why you're there and believing you have something real to offer.

That's the shift this book is about.

CHAPTER 4

THE VOICE IN YOUR HEAD

There's a conversation happening inside you right now. (If you don't think you do, it's the voice that just said, "What? I don't have a voice in my head.")

You may not notice it because it's been running so long that it feels like silence. But if you pause and listen, you'll hear it: a constant stream of commentary, evaluation, prediction, and judgment. It narrates your day. It interprets your interactions. It tells you what things mean, what you're capable of, and what other people are thinking about you.

This internal voice shapes everything about how you show up. And for most people, that voice is not kind.

Randy has spent decades helping people recognize and transform their internal dialogue. He calls the harsh, critical version the "bully voice" and the supportive, compassionate version the "best friend voice," a framework he explores in depth in his book *Becoming Your Own BFF*.[1] These aren't clinical terms.

They're descriptions that people immediately recognize because they've lived with both.

Understanding which voice is running the show and learning to choose differently are among the most practical skills anyone in hospitality can develop. It changes how you experience difficult guests, how you recover from mistakes, how you handle pressure, and ultimately, how sustainable your career in service becomes.

THE VOICE YOU KNOW TOO WELL

Picture this: It's 6:45 a.m. You're in the break room, pouring your first coffee of the day. You slept poorly. Traffic was bad. You're already thinking about the difficult checkout you'll have to handle from last night's complaint.

Now, notice what's happening in your head.

For many people, the internal commentary sounds something like this:

I'm already exhausted, and my shift hasn't even started. This is going to be a disaster. That guest is going to be impossible. Why do I always get the difficult ones? I'm not equipped for this today. Everyone else seems to handle these situations better than I do. What if I say the wrong thing and make it worse? My supervisor is already watching me after last week ...

This is the "bully voice." It's the internal narrator that assumes the worst, magnifies problems, compares you unfavorably to others, and predicts failure. It speaks in absolutes: always, never, everyone, no one. It treats mistakes as evidence of fundamental inadequacy rather than normal human experiences.

The "bully voice" isn't out to hurt you, exactly. In some twisted way, it thinks it's protecting you. By anticipating everything that could go wrong, it believes it's keeping you prepared. By reminding you of your shortcomings, it thinks it's motivating you to do better. By comparing you to others, it imagines it's giving you useful information.

But the effect is the opposite. The "bully voice" is the killer of confidence and self-esteem. It drains energy, increases anxiety, and makes the very failures it predicts more likely. When you're spending mental resources defending yourself against your own internal critic, you have less attention available for the actual human being in front of you.

THE VOICE YOU DESERVE

Now imagine that same morning, same circumstances, but with a different internal narrator.

Okay, rough night. Rough morning. That happens sometimes. The checkout situation might be challenging, but I've handled difficult guests before. I don't have to be perfect. I just need to be present and do my best. If it goes sideways, I'll figure it out. I have support if I need it.

This is the "best friend voice." It's the internal narrator that acknowledges reality without catastrophizing, that recognizes difficulty without predicting doom, that holds you accountable without attacking your worth.

Notice what the "best friend voice" doesn't do: It doesn't pretend everything is fine. It doesn't engage in toxic positivity. It doesn't tell you to just smile and push through. It tells you the truth, but with kindness.

The "best friend voice" is what you'd say to a close friend in the same situation. If a colleague came to you at 6:45 a.m., clearly exhausted and worried about a difficult checkout, you wouldn't say, "Yeah, you're probably going to blow it. You always struggle with these situations." You'd offer perspective, encouragement, and practical support.

We're often far kinder to others than we are to ourselves. The work is learning to extend that same kindness inward.

HOW THE VOICES SHOW UP IN SERVICE

The internal voice doesn't stay internal. It leaks into every interaction, shaping tone, body language, and the subtle energy that guests sense without knowing why.

Remember the ego vs. self-esteem continuum from chapter 3? This is where it lives in real time. The "bully voice" is ego talking: protective, reactive, and focused on how things look. The "best friend voice" is self-esteem talking: grounded, present, and focused on what's actually happening. Watch what changes depending on which one is running the show.

Let's trace how the same situation plays out differently depending on which voice is running.

The situation: A guest approaches, looking frustrated. They've been waiting fifteen minutes for their car from the valet.

"Bully voice" internal experience:
Great, another angry guest. They're going to yell at me, and it's not even my fault. The valet team is so slow today. Why do I have to deal with their mistakes? This person already looks like they're going to be difficult. I need to get them out of here before my manager sees this. Don't mess this up.

"Bully voice" external response:
"I apologize for the wait. Let me check on your car right now."

The words are fine. The script is followed. But the guest senses something: the slight tension in the shoulders, the defensive undertone in the voice, the feeling that they're being managed rather than helped. The interaction resolves, but it leaves a residue of dissatisfaction.

"Best friend voice" internal experience:
This person is frustrated. Fifteen minutes is a long time to wait when you're ready to go. This isn't about me. Let me see what's happening and whether I can help move things along. If I stay calm, that might help them feel calmer, too.

"Best friend voice" external response:
"Fifteen minutes is a long time to wait. I'm sorry about that. Let me find out exactly where things stand and see if I can speed this up for you."

Similar words. Different energy. The guest feels heard rather than handled. They sense that the person helping them is genuinely present and on their side rather than defending against an attack.

This is the difference that guests experience but often don't name. They'll say things like "The staff was so friendly" or "Everyone was really helpful" without being able to pinpoint exactly what made it feel that way. Often, what they're responding to is the quality of presence that comes when someone isn't fighting an internal battle while working to serve them.

COMMON "BULLY VOICE" PATTERNS

The "bully voice" has favorite scripts. Learning to recognize them is the first step toward choosing differently.

The Catastrophizer takes any problem and projects it to its worst possible outcome. A minor complaint becomes evidence that you're going to be fired. A difficult morning becomes proof that the entire day is ruined.

Then there's **the Comparator**, constantly measuring you against others and finding you lacking. That colleague who seems to handle everything effortlessly. The team member who never seems stressed. The comparison is always unfair because you're comparing your insides to their outsides.

The Mind Reader claims to know what others are thinking, and it's never good. Your supervisor's glance means they're disappointed in you. The guest's tone means they think you're incompetent. The coworker's silence means they're upset with you.

You might recognize **the Perfectionist** who sets impossible standards and then punishes you for failing to meet them.

Nothing is ever good enough. Success is dismissed, but failures are cataloged and replayed.

The Historian maintains a detailed record of every mistake you've ever made and brings them up at the worst possible moments. That time three years ago when you handled something poorly? It's still relevant, apparently.

And finally, **the Fortune Teller** predicts failure with great confidence. You'll definitely mess this up. They'll certainly be disappointed. This will absolutely go wrong.

Do any of these sound familiar? Most people have a primary pattern, and recognizing yours makes it easier to catch the voice in action.

WHY THE "BULLY VOICE" IS SO LOUD

So, why does the "bully voice" stick around?

There are a few reasons.

Many of us learned it young. We internalized critical voices from parents, teachers, coaches, or peers. The "bully voice" often sounds like someone from our past, someone whose approval we wanted and whose criticism we feared. Long after that person's actual presence in our lives has diminished, their voice continues to run through our heads.

The "bully voice" genuinely believes it's helping. From its perspective, if it can anticipate every possible failure, you'll be prepared. If it can keep you humble, you won't take risks that might embarrass you. If it can remind you of past mistakes, you won't repeat them. This is misguided logic, but it's not malicious.

The "bully voice" is reinforced by cultural messages. We're taught that high standards require harsh self-criticism. That success demands relentless self-improvement. That ease is suspicious, and struggle is virtuous. The "bully voice" feels like the responsible, mature approach. The "best friend voice" can feel like letting yourself off the hook.

But the research tells a different story. Psychologist Kristin Neff's work on self-compassion shows it's associated with greater resilience, better performance under pressure, and faster recovery from setbacks.[2,3] People who treat themselves kindly don't achieve less. They achieve more sustainably, without the burnout that accompanies constant self-criticism.

BUILDING YOUR "BEST FRIEND VOICE"

Developing a kinder internal voice is about building an alternative that becomes increasingly available over time. You're not silencing the "bully voice" through force. That rarely works and often backfires (the bully just gets louder when attacked).

The Best Friend Test

When you notice harsh self-talk, ask: "Would I say this to a friend in the same situation?"

If the answer is no, that's useful information. It means you're holding yourself to a standard of negativity you'd never apply to someone you care about. Then ask: "What would I say to a friend?" That's your "best friend voice." Use those words on yourself.

This sounds simple, but at first it can be a difficult transition. Once you do, it's surprisingly powerful. Most people discover a dramatic gap between how they speak to themselves and how they speak to others. Closing that gap is the work that brings an incredible sense of relief, confidence, and joy.

Catching and Naming

The "bully voice" thrives on going unnoticed. When it operates below conscious awareness, it feels like the truth rather than one possible interpretation.

Start noticing when the voice is running. You might even name it: "There's the catastrophizer again" or "I'm doing the comparison thing." This creates a small but crucial distance between you and the voice. You stop being the voice and start being the one who notices the voice. From that observer position, you have more choice about whether to believe it.

The Reframe

When you catch a "bully voice" statement, practice reframing it in "best friend voice" terms. Find a version of the truth that's accurate but not cruel.

"I always mess this up" becomes "I've struggled with this before, and I'm still learning, but it's definitely better than it used to be."

"Everyone handles this better than me" becomes "Some people find this easier than I do. That's okay. We all have different strengths."

"This is going to be a disaster" becomes "This might be challenging. I'll do my best and see what happens. I know I can always ask Sue for help if I need it."

The reframe doesn't deny difficulty. It just refuses to add unnecessary suffering.

The Pause

Between a triggering situation and your response, there's a space. In that space, you have a choice. Most of the time, we blow past that space so fast we don't even notice it. The "bully voice" fills it with automatic reactions before we can think.

Practice pausing. When you feel triggered (chest tightens, stomach drops, face flushes), take one breath before responding. Just one. In that breath, you can notice which voice is running and choose whether to let it drive.

This is simple but not easy. It requires practice, just like walking or memorizing the alphabet. You don't remember how many times you fell when you were learning how to walk. No one just stands up the first time and dashes across the room. But over time and with lots of practice and encouragement, you learned to walk. Now it's so easy you don't even think about it. You just do it. Learning to pause or shift to the "best friend voice" is the same.

The Voice Check-In

One practice that works well is a regular "voice check-in." This could be part of your routine throughout the day.

The question is simple: "Which voice is louder?"

You don't need to get into details. Just an honest acknowledgment: "My 'bully voice' was pretty active this morning, but it's better than it was yesterday!" or "I'm in a decent headspace. I'm using my 'best friend' voice more often."

With practice and attention, you'll notice a definite shift until the "best friend voice" becomes the dominant voice you're listening to. Sure, the bully rears its head every now and then, but with less frequency and volume.

The goal isn't to eliminate the "bully voice." It will always be there. The goal is to build the "best friend voice" strong enough that you have a choice about which one to listen to.

FROM INDIVIDUAL TO TEAM

When individuals start managing their internal dialogue more skillfully, something shifts at the team level, too.

A team where everyone is constantly running internal criticism is operating from collective depletion. People are guarded, defensive, and quick to blame. Mistakes get hidden rather than addressed. Feedback feels like an attack.

A team where multiple people have developed their "best friend voice" is different. There's more grace for imperfection. Mistakes become learning rather than shame. People are more willing to take risks because they're not terrified of failure. The psychological safety that's so important for service excellence becomes more possible when people aren't already at war with themselves.

The internal voice work isn't just personal development. It's a team performance strategy. It starts with leaders who are willing to do their own work and model a different way of relating to themselves.

THE RIPPLE EFFECT

The internal voice doesn't stay internal.

The way you talk to yourself becomes the way you talk to others. Leaders who are harsh with themselves tend to be harsh with their teams. Team members who constantly criticize themselves have less patience for colleagues' imperfections.

The reverse is also true. When you develop compassion for your own struggles, you naturally extend more compassion to others. When you stop expecting perfection from yourself, you stop demanding it from everyone around you.

The "best friend voice" isn't just about feeling better. It's about becoming better at the actual work of hospitality, which requires patience, presence, and the ability to meet imperfect humans (including yourself) with grace.

The voice in your head shapes the experience guests have with you. When that voice is kind, your service carries a different quality. When that voice is cruel, no amount of script-following covers it completely.

The good news is that you have more control over that voice than you might think. It's not total control or immediate transformation, but it's the capacity to notice, pause, choose, and, over time, build an internal narrator who supports rather than sabotages you.

That's the foundation on which everything else in this book builds.

CHAPTER 5

THE ENERGY BALL

In chapter 2, we explored the external forces that drain your energy ball: difficult guests, toxic colleagues, broken systems, and the life circumstances you carry with you to every shift. Now let's look at how to recognize when your ball is shrinking, what actually fills it back up, and what you might be doing to drain it yourself.

This might be the most practical chapter in the book. The internal voice work matters. The worth foundation matters. But if you're running on empty, none of that knowledge helps you in the moment when a guest needs you to be present, and you have nothing left to give.

Energy management isn't a luxury. For people in service roles, it's essential.

WHAT THE ENERGY BALL ACTUALLY IS

Let's be more precise about what we mean by "energy" in this context.

We're not talking about physical energy alone, though that's part of it. We're talking about your overall capacity for engaged, authentic presence. Your ability to show up fully rather than going through the motions. The difference between being at work and being present at work.

This capacity draws from multiple sources: physical (how rested, nourished, and cared for your body is), mental (how clear or cluttered your thinking is), emotional (how processed or overwhelming your feelings are), and spiritual (how connected or disconnected you feel from meaning and purpose).

We'll explore each of these dimensions in detail in Part Three. For now, think of your energy ball as the combined total of all four. When any one dimension is depleted, the whole ball shrinks. When one or more are resourced, the ball expands.

The beach ball state feels like ease, patience, genuine interest in others, ability to handle surprises, creative problem-solving, natural warmth, an easy laugh, and a genuine smile.

The marble state feels like irritation, impatience, going through motions, dreading interactions, inability to think clearly, and forcing a smile that doesn't reach your eyes.

Most people don't operate at the extremes. They live somewhere in the middle, fluctuating throughout the day, the week, the season. The goal isn't to maintain beach ball energy at all times. That's not realistic. The goal is to understand what affects your energy, notice when it's dropping, and have strategies for both protecting and restoring it.

THE SIGNALS YOUR BODY SENDS

Your energy ball doesn't shrink silently. Your body sends signals. The problem is that most of us have learned to ignore them.

Physical signals:

- You notice tension in your shoulders, neck, or jaw.
- You're breathing shallowly or holding your breath.
- You feel fatigue that doesn't match how much you slept.
- You get headaches or digestive discomfort that seem to come from nowhere.

Mental signals:

- You have difficulty concentrating or a fog you cannot shake.
- You notice forgetfulness (where did I put that? what was I doing?).
- Your thoughts are racing and won't settle.
- Tasks that are usually manageable feel overwhelming.

Emotional signals:

- You feel irritability out of proportion to what triggered it.
- You're close to tears without a clear cause, or you feel numb.
- You experience free-floating anxiety without a clear source.
- You feel a strong urge to hide or escape.

Spiritual signals:

- You feel disconnected from people you're usually close to.
- You find yourself thinking, "What's the point?"
- You feel like an outsider, even with your own team.
- Conversations or interactions you'd normally enjoy hold no interest.

Behavioral signals:

- You start withdrawing from colleagues or avoiding interactions you'd usually welcome.
- Your responses are shorter than usual.
- You begin clock-watching.
- You find yourself cutting corners you wouldn't normally cut.

These signals are information. They're telling you something about your energy state before you hit the wall. The earlier you notice them, the more options you have for responding.

Most people don't notice until they're already at marble size, and by then, the options are limited. Learning to catch the signals earlier is one of the most valuable skills you can develop. If you put out the fire on your stove top, it's a simple task. If you ignore it, the fire engulfs the kitchen and, eventually, your entire house.

WHAT FILLS THE BALL

Before we name the drains, it's worth knowing what makes the ball grow. Understanding your personal sources of replenishment is essential because once you know what fills you, the drains stop feeling like the only force at work.

The tricky part is that what fills one person's ball might drain another's. This is highly individual. Some people recharge through social connection; others need solitude. Some people find physical activity energizing; others find it depleting. Some people are restored by nature; others, by urban environments.

A few common categories worth exploring:

Rest: This is not just sleep, though sleep is foundational, but genuine rest. Allow for moments where nothing is being demanded of you, where you're not producing, performing, or responding. This could be anything from a fifteen-minute power nap to sitting quietly in the break room with your eyes closed, listening to meditative music, to maintaining a solid sleep schedule. For many people in service roles, this kind of rest is rare but essential. And without quality rest or downtime, the ball never fully reinflates.

Connection: Genuine human connection, not transactional interaction, but real contact with people who see you, is restorative for most people. This might be friends, family, colleagues you trust, or even brief moments of authentic exchange with strangers. The keyword is *genuine*. Shallow socializing can actually drain rather than fill.

Movement: Bodies that don't move become sluggish. The right kind of physical activity can quickly shift your energy state. This doesn't have to mean intense exercise. A walk, stretching, dancing in your kitchen. Whatever gets you out of your head and into your body.

Nature: There's something about being in natural environments that restores many people at a deep level. Even brief exposure (a few minutes outside, a plant on your desk, a window with a view of trees) can help. If you work in an environment with no natural elements, it's important to be more intentional about seeking them during breaks and off-hours.

Creative expression: Making something (art, music, food, writing, crafts, gardens) fills the ball in a way that consumption doesn't. The act of creating seems to generate energy rather than just using it.

Meaning: Connecting to purpose, to something larger than yourself, is energizing. This might be spiritual practice, volunteer work, or simply remembering why your work matters. The meaning chapter, chapter 9, will explore this further.

Pleasure: Seek out simple enjoyment. These are things that feel good without requiring justification, such as a hot bath, a favorite meal, listening to music you love, or planning a weekend getaway. We often feel guilty about pleasure, as if we should be doing something more productive. But pleasure is productive. It restores capacity. Engage in pursuits that are fun for you, and make time to prioritize them.

The invitation is to get curious about what actually fills your energy ball, not what you think should fill it, or what fills other people's. Experiment. Pay attention. Build a personal menu of restoration options to draw from when you notice your energy dropping.

WHAT DRAINS THE BALL

Knowing what fills the ball matters. Knowing what drains it matters, too, because even the best restoration practices can't keep up with depletion you don't see coming.

In chapter 2, we covered energy vampires: external forces (difficult guests, toxic colleagues, broken systems) and life circumstances (financial stress, family challenges, health concerns) that drain your reserves. But there's another category of drain that deserves attention: self-inflicted depletion.

The "bully voice" is a constant drain. Every time your internal critic runs its script (you're not good enough, you're going to fail, everyone is judging you), it costs energy. The mental work of defending yourself against your own attacks is exhausting. The voice work in chapter 4 matters for energy management: A kinder internal voice is literally less draining.

Resistance consumes enormous energy. Fighting against reality does, too. When you spend your shift wishing things were different (wishing this guest wasn't so difficult, wishing you weren't so tired, wishing your coworker would do their job), you're burning fuel on something that changes nothing. Acceptance isn't the same as approval. It just means stopping the energy bleed of constant resistance.

Maintaining a false front is exhausting. When there's a significant gap between how you actually feel and how you're presenting, that gap has to be managed constantly. Authentic service is actually less tiring than mechanical service: You're not spending energy maintaining a performance when you're being authentic.

Rumination drains energy without giving anything back. Replaying past interactions, rehearsing future conversations, or worrying about things you cannot control is mental activity that feels productive (You're preparing! You're processing!), but mostly it's just expensive. The energy goes out, and nothing useful comes back.

Poor boundaries come with an energy tax. Every time you say yes when you mean no, every time you take on something that isn't yours to carry, every time you let someone cross a line you should have held, you pay an energy tax. Poor boundaries are one of the most common sources of chronic depletion in service roles.

Noticing your self-inflicted drains is empowering, not shaming. You cannot control the difficult guest. You can control how long you replay the interaction afterward.

ENERGY MANAGEMENT DURING A SHIFT

Knowing what drains and fills your energy ball is useful for long-term sustainability. But what about during a shift, when you're stuck at work, your energy is dropping, and you don't have access to most of your restoration options?

Here are some in-the-moment strategies:

Two-Minute Reset: When you notice your energy flagging, take two minutes (set a timer if needed) to do something purely restorative. Step outside. Splash water on your face. Do some deep breaths. Stretch. Look out a window. Listen to one song. Two minutes isn't long, but it's enough to interrupt the depletion spiral.

Bathroom Break Boundary: The bathroom is often the only truly private space available during a shift. Use it not just for biological needs but for brief mental resets. Even ninety seconds of closed eyes and deep breathing can shift your state.

Micro-Connection: A brief moment of genuine connection with a colleague can fill the ball slightly. Not venting (that often drains both people), but actual connection. A shared joke. A moment of real eye contact. A hug from a trusted friend. An acknowledgment that you see each other as humans, not just coworkers.

Body Scan: When you notice depletion signals, take thirty seconds to scan your body. Where are you holding tension? Shoulders tight? Jaw clenched? Stomach knotted? Notice where you're bracing. Then consciously release it. Are you breathing shallowly? Take three deep breaths. This doesn't solve the underlying drain, but it stops the physical tension from accelerating the depletion.

Perspective Shift: When you're in marble territory, everything feels hard, and nothing feels worth it. A brief perspective shift can help. Ask yourself: "What's one good thing about right now?" or "What will I be glad I did when this shift is over?" This isn't toxic positivity. It's just interrupting the tunnel vision that comes with depletion.

Strategic Sequence: If you have any control over the order of your tasks, put something energizing (or at least neutral) after something draining. Completed a difficult interaction? Pause to acknowledge what you accomplished. Let yourself feel proud, even if the win feels small. Follow it with a task you enjoy or find easy. This prevents the accumulation effect, where one hard thing leads directly to another.

WHEN YOU HIT MARBLE SIZE

Sometimes, despite your best efforts, you hit bottom. The ball is marble-sized. You have nothing left, and you still have hours remaining in your shift.

First, this happens to everyone. It's not a character flaw. It's not proof that you're bad at your job or lack resilience. It's the natural consequence of being human in demanding circumstances.

Second, marble-size energy is a signal that something needs to change. If you're hitting marble regularly, that's information about either your circumstances (too many drains, not enough restoration) or your boundaries (taking on more than you can sustain). The immediate crisis needs to be handled, but the pattern needs to be addressed.

In the immediate crisis:

Ask for help. If you have colleagues or supervisors you trust, this is the time to put that trust to use. "I'm really struggling right now. Can you cover me for ten minutes?" or "I need to tap out of that difficult situation. Can you take it?" Asking for help isn't weakness. It's wisdom.

Protect the guest. When you're depleted, you're more likely to snap, make mistakes, or communicate irritation you don't intend. The guest doesn't deserve that. If you feel yourself about to say or do something you'll regret, pause. Take a breath. If necessary, excuse yourself briefly. "Let me check on that for you," buys you thirty seconds to collect yourself.

Don't make it worse. When you're at marble size, avoid decisions you'll regret. Don't send that email. Don't have that conversation with your supervisor. Don't quit your job (at least not today). *Marble-size energy produces marble-size judgment.* Wait until you've recovered before making choices that matter.

THE RECOVERY CONVERSATION

After you've hit marble size and made it through, there's important work to do.

Acknowledge what happened, not with shame, but with honesty. "I was really depleted today. My energy hit bottom around 2 p.m., and I was just surviving after that."

Get curious about why. What drained you to that point? Was it accumulated stress over days or weeks? Was it a specific incident that tipped you over? Was it inadequate recovery from a previous depletion? Or would an afternoon snack help boost your energy? Understanding the cause helps you prevent recurrence.

Assess your recovery resources. Are your current strategies actually working? Do you have enough restoration options? Are you using them? Often, people know what fills their ball but don't prioritize it. This is where the "best friend voice" matters: It gives you permission to take care of yourself.

Consider what needs to change. If marble-size depletion is a regular occurrence, something about your circumstances or your approach isn't sustainable. This might mean taking better care of physical, mental, or emotional needs. Having conversations about workload, schedule changes, boundary adjustments, or even bigger questions about whether this role is right for you.

Energy rises and falls. That's natural. The goal isn't to never hit marble size again. The goal is awareness: noticing when you're approaching depletion, catching it early, looking for patterns, and recovering fully when it happens.

ENERGY AS A TEAM RESPONSIBILITY

So far, we've focused on individual energy management. But in a team environment, energy is also a collective responsibility.

Teams can protect each other's energy: noticing when a colleague is flailing, offering support before it's requested, covering for each other during rough patches, and celebrating wins together.

Teams can also drain each other's energy: complaining constantly, creating drama, failing to pull their weight, and bringing negative energy into shared spaces.

Leaders have a particular responsibility here. They set the tone for whether energy management is valued or dismissed. They create (or fail to create) systems that support sustainability. They model either a burnout culture (always on, never resting, treating exhaustion as a badge of honor) or a healthy work culture (taking breaks, acknowledging limits, prioritizing recovery).

The question worth asking about any team practice is: Does this fill or drain the collective energy ball? Meetings, communication patterns, scheduling decisions, and feedback approaches: All of these either support or undermine the team's capacity for sustained excellent service.

Energy management is a daily practice, but it's also a long game.

Short-term, you're hoping to get through each shift with enough left to be present for guests and for your own life afterward.

Medium-term, you're working to prevent the slow dim described in chapter 2, the gradual depletion that turns engaged employees into those who are burned-out.

Long-term, you're striving to build a career in hospitality that's sustainable across years and decades. That requires not just surviving individual shifts but creating patterns of work and recovery that can be maintained over time.

The people who last in this industry, who still love it after twenty or thirty years, have figured out energy management. Not perfectly. Not without difficult stretches. But well enough to keep their ball inflated enough, often enough, to sustain genuine presence.

That's the goal. Not beach ball energy every moment (impossible), but a sustainable rhythm that keeps you out of marble territory most of the time and helps you recover quickly when you do hit bottom.

Your energy ball is your most valuable professional (and personal) resource. Treat it that way.

Randy Remembers: Before the Rush

In hospitality, the holiday season is predictably stressful. The pace increases, guests are more demanding, and everyone's running on less rest. Most people don't prepare for it until they're already in it.

Randy learned the value of early preparation in an unexpected place. Years ago, he worked in a counseling center doing group therapy for adults who grew up in households affected by addiction. Every year, he noticed the same pattern: As the holidays approached, his clients became more agitated. Family gatherings meant old dynamics, old triggers, sometimes old temptations. The first year, he didn't recognize what was happening until November, when the stress was already building. The following year, he started preparing them in September. They talked about recognizing early warning signs, identifying triggers, and building strategies to get through the season without accumulating new damage.

The same principle applies in hospitality. If you know a difficult period is coming, don't wait until you're in it to start managing your energy. Prepare early and build your reserves. Anticipate what will drain the team and plan accordingly. The teams that do this experience the holiday rush as demanding but manageable. The teams that don't are running on empty by December 15.

PART THREE

CARING FOR THE WHOLE PERSON

Your energy ball draws from four sources. Neglect any one of them, and the whole system suffers. Resource all four, and they reinforce each other in ways that multiply your capacity for genuine presence.

Randy's framework identifies these four dimensions as physical, mental, emotional, and spiritual. They're not separate compartments. They're interconnected aspects of one whole person. Examining them individually helps us understand what each needs and what happens when any are depleted.

In the chapters that follow, we'll explore each dimension: what it contributes to your capacity for service, what drains it, what fills it, and practical strategies for keeping it resourced.

We start with the physical, not because it's most important, but because it's foundational. When the body is depleted, everything else becomes more difficult.

CHAPTER 6

PHYSICAL— THE FOUNDATION EVERYTHING ELSE RESTS ON

Sara has been a housekeeper at the resort for six years. She takes pride in her work. Guests have written comment cards specifically praising the care she puts into room presentation, the small touches she adds, and the way everything feels fresh and cared-for when she's finished.

But today is different.

She's on room fourteen of a sixteen-room day. Her lower back seized up around room eight, that familiar grinding pain she's learned to work through. Her feet feel like they're wrapped in sandpaper. She skipped lunch again because there wasn't time, and the protein bar she grabbed from her locker three hours ago has long since burned off.

She's standing in the bathroom of room fourteen, looking at the shower that needs scrubbing, and something in her just ... stops.

It's not that she doesn't care. She does. That's almost the problem. She remembers when this work felt meaningful, when finishing a room gave her genuine satisfaction. Now she's just hoping to make it to the end of her shift without crying or screaming or walking out.

The guest who checks into this room tonight will receive adequate service. The room will be clean. The standards will be met. But the thing that made Sara's rooms special, that extra attention, that pride, that invisible care guests couldn't name but definitely felt? That's not available today. Sara doesn't have access to it right now.

She's not lazy. She's not disengaged. She's physically depleted, making everything else much more difficult.

THE INVISIBLE WEIGHT

Physical depletion is the most overlooked factor in service quality.

We talk endlessly about attitude, training, motivation, and engagement. We measure customer satisfaction, create recognition programs, and hold team meetings about service excellence. But we rarely talk about the simple fact that human bodies have limits, and when those limits are exceeded, nothing else works the way it's supposed to.

Hospitality work is physically demanding in ways that don't always get acknowledged. You spend hours on your feet, often engaging in repetitive motions. Irregular schedules disrupt sleep. Meals are grabbed on the run or skipped entirely. You're exposed to temperature extremes as you move between kitchens, outdoor venues, and walk-in freezers. You're lifting, carrying, bending, and reaching.

The cumulative effect of this physical demand shows up in tired bodies and in diminished capacity for everything else. When you're physically exhausted:

- Your cognitive function declines. Decision-making becomes harder. You're more likely to make mistakes, forget things, and miss details.
- Your emotional regulation suffers. You have less patience. Things that wouldn't normally bother you become irritating. Your fuse shortens.
- Your ability to connect diminishes. Genuine presence requires energy. When your body is screaming for rest, you don't have attention left over for the subtle work of human connection.
- Your "bully voice" gets louder. Physical depletion makes everything feel harder. The internal critic has more ammunition when you're exhausted.

Physical wellness isn't a nice-to-have or a personal lifestyle choice. For people in service roles, it's a professional capacity issue. Depleted bodies produce depleted service.

WHAT BUILDS PHYSICAL CAPACITY

The foundations are simple and well-known. That doesn't make them easy to implement, especially in an industry that often works against them.

Sleep: This is foundational, as everything else depends on it. Chronic sleep deprivation degrades every other system: cognitive, emotional, physical, and immune. Most adults need seven to nine hours. Most hospitality workers get less, often much less. Shift work, irregular schedules, and the adrenaline of demanding days conspire to undermine adequate rest.

The research on sleep deprivation is sobering. A study published in *Occupational and Environmental Medicine* found that after seventeen to nineteen hours without sleep, cognitive and motor performance is equivalent to a blood alcohol level of 0.05%.[1] After longer periods, it's equivalent to legal intoxication. We would never ask team members to serve guests while drunk, but we routinely ask them to serve guests while sleep-deprived.

Nourishment: Bodies need fuel. Not just calories, but actual nutrition. The pattern of skipping meals, relying on caffeine and sugar to push through, and grabbing whatever's fast and available is endemic in hospitality. It's also a recipe for energy crashes, mood instability, and long-term health consequences.

Eating well in a hospitality environment can be challenging. Break times are unpredictable. Healthy options aren't always available. The temptation to just power through is strong. But the cost of chronic poor nutrition shows up in service quality, even when no one names it as the cause.

Hydration: Dehydration affects cognitive function before you feel thirsty. By the time you notice you need water, your performance has already declined. In busy service environments, it's easy to go hours without drinking anything. Making hydration automatic (water bottle always accessible, drinking at set times) helps counter this.

Movement and rest: The physical demands of hospitality work provide plenty of movement for most roles, but it's often repetitive movement that stresses some systems while neglecting others. Intentional movement that stretches, strengthens, and balances the body helps prevent injury and maintain capacity. Randy knew team members who would walk around the property together for ten minutes during their lunch break.

Rest is equally important. Not just sleep, but actual recovery time. Hospitality schedules often don't support this. Back-to-back shifts, unpredictable days off, and the expectation of constant availability: All of these prevent true physical recovery. Randy experienced this in one of his guest services roles, where he interacted with one guest after another for hours at a time. During breaks, he would sit quietly in the break room, not because he was antisocial or ignoring people. He was reserving and replenishing his energy for the rest of his shift.

Pain and injury attention: Hospitality work is associated with injuries: repetitive stress, prolonged standing, accidents, and the cumulative effects of physical labor. There's often a culture of "pushing through" pain, treating it as a badge of honor rather than a signal that something needs attention.

Unaddressed pain is an energy drain that never stops. It diverts attention, disrupts sleep, degrades mood, and makes every other demand feel harder. Getting treatment, making ergonomic adjustments, and taking injuries seriously aren't signs of weakness. It's maintenance of your primary professional tool: your body.

WHAT DRAINS PHYSICAL CAPACITY

Some drains are obvious: inadequate sleep, poor nutrition, injury, and illness. Others are less visible.

Chronic stress: The body's stress response is designed for short-term threats. When stress becomes chronic, the physical toll accumulates. Elevated cortisol, disrupted sleep, suppressed immune function, and muscle tension that never fully releases. Chronic stress is physically expensive. Research shows prolonged cortisol elevation suppresses immune function, disrupts sleep architecture, and accelerates cellular aging.[2]

Environmental factors: Temperature extremes, poor air quality, inadequate lighting, and excessive noise: All of these stress the body. Many hospitality environments involve at least some of these challenges. Where they're addressable, addressing them is an investment in team capacity.

Insufficient recovery between shifts: The body needs time to repair. When shifts are scheduled too close together, or when people pick up extra shifts to make ends meet, recovery doesn't happen. The cumulative effect is a body that's always running at a deficit.

Self-neglect: Under pressure, self-care is often the first thing sacrificed. Skip the workout. Increase alcohol consumption. Grab fast food instead of cooking. Stay up late because it's the only personal time available. Ignore the warning signs because there's no time to address them. Each choice seems minor. The cumulative effect is significant.

SMALL SHIFTS, REAL DIFFERENCES

Transforming physical wellness doesn't require a complete life overhaul. Small, consistent shifts often matter more than dramatic interventions.

Sleep support: Even if you don't get more hours, you can get better quality with some simple fixes. Consider sleeping in a dark room, keeping your bedroom cool, maintaining a consistent schedule (as much as possible), turning off screens before bed, and avoiding caffeine, alcohol, and snacks a couple of hours before bedtime. These small adjustments can vastly improve sleep quality even when quantity is constrained.

Strategic eating: If full meals aren't possible, strategic snacking helps. Eating foods with protein and complex carbs provides sustained energy more than foods with empty calories and lots of sugar. Keeping healthy options accessible in your locker, your car, or your bag makes good choices easier when time is short.

Protein bars with high protein and low sugar are great options for afternoon snacks.

Hydration habits: Make it automatic. Always have a water bottle with you. Drink every time you complete a task or take a break. Set reminders if needed. The goal is to remove the decision so hydration happens without requiring willpower. The goal is half your body weight in ounces (if you weigh 100 pounds, drink 50 ounces of water per day).

Micro-recovery: Even brief physical recovery matters: sitting for two minutes after standing for a few hours, stretching for thirty seconds between tasks, or closing your eyes for one minute (preferably in the break room, not on the floor). These micro-breaks don't solve chronic depletion, but they prevent the acceleration that happens when physical stress goes completely uninterrupted.

Pain attention: Take the ibuprofen when the headache or pain starts. Wear compression socks or the back brace. See a physical therapist if the pain becomes chronic. Address the small issues before they become big ones. This isn't complaining or weakness. It's professional maintenance.

THE ORGANIZATIONAL DIMENSION

Individual choices matter, but so do organizational practices. Some physical depletion is self-inflicted. Some is structurally imposed.

Schedules that don't always allow for adequate recovery between shifts, workloads that make breaks impossible, environments that are too hot, too cold, or too loud, lack of access to healthy food options, and pressure to work while sick or injured are all organizational choices that affect teams' physical capacity.

Leaders who want their teams to deliver excellent service need to examine whether their practices support or undermine physical wellness. This isn't just about being nice to employees (though it is that, too). It's about creating conditions where excellent service is actually possible.

A few questions to think about:

- Do our schedules allow adequate recovery time between shifts?
- Do team members actually take their breaks, or is the workload structured such that breaks are technically available but practically impossible?
- What food and hydration options are accessible during shifts?
- How do we handle requests for time off due to illness or injury?
- What is our actual (not stated) culture around physical self-care?

The answers reveal whether the organization is a partner in physical wellness or an obstacle to it.

PHYSICAL WELLNESS AND SERVICE QUALITY

The connection between physical wellness and service quality is direct, even when it's invisible.

Doesn't it make sense that a team member who slept well, ate well, isn't in pain, and has had adequate recovery time shows up differently than one who is sleep-deprived, hungry, hurting, and exhausted? The difference may not be obvious in any single interaction, but across hundreds of interactions per day, across an entire team, across weeks and months, it's enormous.

Investment in physical wellness is an investment in service quality, not as a perk or a nice gesture, but as a business strategy.

The guest doesn't know that Maria has a headache. They don't know that James skipped breakfast. They don't know that Sara's back is seizing up. But they feel the effect. They experience service that's slightly less warm, slightly less attentive, slightly less magical. They may not be able to name what's missing, but something is.

Physical wellness isn't separate from service excellence. It's the foundation that makes service excellence possible.

Sara, in room fourteen, with her back screaming as her blood sugar crashed, and two more rooms to go: She's not capable of delivering her best work right now. Not because she doesn't want to. Not because she lacks training, motivation, or commitment. Because her body is telling her the truth: There's nothing left to give.

The question isn't how to motivate Sara to push through. The question is how we got here in the first place and what would need to change so that Sara's body is resourced enough to support the excellent work she's capable of doing.

From Both of Us: The Shoes and the Fall

Randy learned this lesson early. Before starting his first role at Disney, where he'd be standing for eight hours a shift, he went to a local shoe store and asked for their best shoe for someone on their feet all day. The clerk immediately pointed at one. It was a little more expensive than the others, but he knew it was an investment. He bought two pairs.

Kat learned it the hard way.

Early in her career, in her first management position, she put so much pressure on herself that she'd forget to eat. She wouldn't ask for help because she feared it would make her look like she didn't have things under control. During the first big event she led, she fainted. She hit the ground and got right back up, even as colleagues looked on with concern. That night, she went home with a migraine that knocked her flat.

All that worry and fear of failure had been stored in her body with nowhere else to go. She hadn't asked for help. She hadn't shown vulnerability. She wasn't there yet.

Two approaches. One proactive, one learned through pain. Either way, the body keeps score.

CHAPTER 7

MENTAL—CLEAR THINKING UNDER PRESSURE

It's 2:47 p.m., and David is standing at the front desk.

The phone is ringing. A guest is waiting in front of him wanting to ask a question. His manager just walked through the lobby and made eye contact in that way that means "I'm watching." A notification just popped up on his screen about a VIP arrival in twenty minutes that he hasn't prepped for. Behind him, a colleague is asking where the extra key cards are stored. Somewhere in the back of his mind, he can't remember if he submitted his schedule request for next month or just thought about submitting it.

His brain feels like a browser with forty-seven tabs open, all of them demanding attention, none of them fully loaded.

The guest in front of him then asks a simple question: "Is there a good Italian restaurant within walking distance?"

David knows the answer. He's given this recommendation dozens of times. But right now, in this moment, with everything else competing for bandwidth, his mind goes blank. He stares at her for a beat too long. She shifts her weight. He can feel himself starting to sweat.

"Let me ... let me check on that for you," he says, turning to his computer even though he doesn't need to. He just needs a moment for his brain to catch up with his mouth.

This is what mental overload looks like from the inside. And it's constantly happening to your team members.

THE BRAIN'S BANDWIDTH PROBLEM

Your brain has limited processing capacity. That's how brains work. Cognitive scientist George Miller's well-known research found that working memory holds roughly four to seven items at once.[1]

When demands exceed capacity, something has to give. You start dropping things: details forgotten, mistakes made, obvious answers suddenly unavailable. The quality of your thinking degrades. Decision-making becomes slower and worse. Things that would normally be easy become inexplicably difficult.

Hospitality work constantly threatens to overwhelm this capacity.

You're simultaneously processing multiple streams of information: the guest in front of you, the phone ringing, the colleague who needs something, the systems you're navigating, the standards you're supposed to maintain, and the problems from earlier that haven't been resolved.

You're making rapid decisions under pressure: which task to do first, how to respond, which exception to make, when to escalate, and how to prioritize competing demands.

You're tracking invisible information: VIP preferences, ongoing situations, promises made to guests, things you need to follow up on, schedule changes, policy updates.

You're doing all of this while attempting to appear calm, friendly, and fully present for whoever is in front of you.

The mental load of hospitality work is enormous, and it's largely invisible. It doesn't show up on task lists or job descriptions. But it's running constantly, draining cognitive resources that could otherwise be devoted to creative problem-solving and genuine human connection.

WHAT MENTAL OVERLOAD ACTUALLY LOOKS LIKE

David's moment at the front desk, where his mind goes blank on a question he knows the answer to, is one manifestation. There are others.

Decision fatigue: Every decision uses mental energy. By the end of a shift filled with hundreds of small decisions, the ability to make good ones is depleted. That's why people make worse choices late in the day, why they become more impulsive or more passive, and why "I don't care; you decide" becomes the default response.

Tunnel vision: When the brain is overloaded, it narrows its focus to what seems most urgent. This means missing things that aren't directly in front of you: the guest who's been waiting, the detail that doesn't fit, the colleague who needs help, the problem developing in the periphery.

Increased errors: Tired brains make mistakes: wrong room numbers, forgotten requests, miscommunication, and details that fall through cracks. These aren't signs of carelessness. They're symptoms of a system that's exceeded its capacity.

Slower processing: Everything takes longer. Responses that would normally be instant require thought. Simple tasks become effortful. The fluid expertise that usually guides your work becomes halting and uncertain.

Irritability: Mental overload is stressful, and stress makes people irritable. The patience required for good service becomes harder to access. Things that wouldn't normally bother you become frustrating.

Inability to think ahead: When all your capacity is consumed by the present moment, there's nothing left for planning, anticipating, or creative thinking. You become purely reactive, handling whatever's immediately in front of you without the bandwidth to see what's coming or prepare for it.

THE MYTH OF MULTITASKING

Hospitality culture often celebrates multitasking. The ability to juggle multiple demands simultaneously is seen as a core competency, a sign of being good at the job.

Here's the problem: Multitasking, as most people think of it, doesn't actually exist.

What feels like doing multiple things at once is actually rapid task switching. And every switch has a cost. Your brain has to disengage from one context, load another, orient to where you were, and resume. This switching tax accumulates. Research from the American Psychological Association and other sources confirms that multitasking (really task-switching) reduces productivity by up to 40% and increases errors.[2,3]

This doesn't mean you have to do one thing at a time in a hospitality environment. (That's not realistic.) But it does mean understanding the cost of constant switching and, where possible, creating conditions that reduce unnecessary switches.

Batching similar tasks, reducing interruptions, creating focused time for complex work, and finishing one thing before starting another when possible aren't about working harder. They're about working in ways that align with how the brain actually functions.

WHERE THE BANDWIDTH GOES

Beyond the baseline demands of the work, certain factors accelerate mental depletion.

Constant interruption: Every interruption breaks your focus and requires mental energy to recover. In environments with constant interruptions, the cumulative drain is significant. Some interruptions are unavoidable. Others are created by poor systems, unclear protocols, or cultural expectations that everyone should always be available for everything.

Unclear expectations: When you don't know what's expected, you spend mental energy hoping to figure it out. When priorities are ambiguous, you spend energy deciding what matters most. When standards are inconsistent, you spend energy guessing how things will be evaluated. Clarity is a cognitive gift. Ambiguity is a cognitive tax.

Information overload: Too many emails, updates, systems to check, and sources of information compete for attention. The feeling of being behind on information, of missing something important, creates a background anxiety that consumes capacity.

Unfinished tasks: The brain struggles to let go of incomplete tasks. They continue to occupy mental space, nagging for attention, even when you want to focus on something else. The more open loops you're carrying, the less capacity you have for what's in front of you.

Worry and rumination: Mental energy spent replaying past problems or anticipating future ones is energy not available for present demands. The "bully voice" is expensive here: All that internal criticism and catastrophizing uses cognitive resources.

Poor physical state: Mental and physical capacity are deeply connected. Sleep deprivation dramatically degrades cognitive function. Hunger affects concentration. Dehydration impairs thinking. Physical depletion becomes mental depletion.

GETTING IT BACK

Some factors are about reducing drain. Others are about building capacity.

Sleep: We mentioned this in chapter 6, but it bears repeating from a mental perspective. Sleep is when the brain consolidates learning, clears metabolic waste, and restores cognitive function. Chronic sleep deprivation doesn't just make you tired. It makes you cognitively impaired. Protecting sleep is protecting your ability to think clearly.

Focused attention practice: The ability to focus is a skill that develops with practice. Meditation and mindfulness, even for brief periods, train this capacity. So does any activity that requires sustained attention without distraction: reading, crafting, playing an instrument, solving puzzles (doing Sudoku puzzles during Randy's breaks was his "go-to"). In a world designed to fragment attention, deliberately practicing focus builds the muscle.

Cognitive recovery: Just as the body needs rest between physical demands, the mind needs rest between cognitive demands. Breaks that are actually restful (not scrolling on your phone, which is its own form of cognitive demand) allow recovery. Consider staring out a window, taking a walk, or sitting quietly. These feel unproductive but are actually essential for sustained mental performance.

Externalized systems: The brain is a terrible storage device. Using external systems, such as lists, calendars, notes, and reminders, to capture and organize information frees up cognitive capacity for actual thinking. Getting things out of your head and into a trusted system reduces the background noise of struggling to remember everything.

Reduced decision load: Every decision costs energy. Reducing unnecessary decisions preserves capacity for the ones that matter. Routines help: They automate recurring choices so you don't have to think about them. It's why simplified systems and clear protocols support good service: They reduce the cognitive load of figuring things out in the moment.

Boundaries on information intake: Not every email requires immediate attention. Not every update needs to be processed right now. Creating boundaries around when and how you engage with information flow protects cognitive capacity for actual work.

SMALL SHIFTS DURING A SHIFT

You're at work. The demands are what they are. What helps in the moment?

Brain dump: When your head is full of swirling tasks and concerns, take two minutes to write them all down. Just getting them out of your head and onto paper reduces the cognitive load of attempting to track everything internally. You haven't done anything yet, but you've freed up mental space.

Single-task moment: When possible, give yourself permission to focus on just one thing for a few minutes. Close extra browser tabs (mental and literal). Finish one task before starting the next. Even brief periods of single-tasking can be restorative.

As the saying goes, how do you eat an elephant? One bite at a time.

Micro-break: Research from the University of Illinois suggests that brief breaks (even two to three minutes) every half hour or so can significantly reduce mental fatigue and restore focus.[4] Step away from the desk. Look at something distant. Let your mind unfocus for a moment. Then return.

Priority reset: When everything feels equally urgent, pause and ask, "What actually matters most right now?" Often, the feeling of overwhelm comes from treating everything as equally important. Consciously choosing what to focus on (and what to let wait) can cut through the paralysis.

Physical reset: Because mental and physical states are connected, physical interventions affect mental capacity. Taking deep breaths, standing up and stretching, drinking water, and stepping outside for fresh air aren't just physical recovery. They're cognitive recovery.

Completion hit: Finishing something, even something small, provides a cognitive reward. When you're overwhelmed, identify one thing you can complete quickly and do it. The sense of completion provides momentum and clears that task from your mental load.

SYSTEMS THAT SUPPORT CLEAR THINKING

Individual strategies help, but organizational systems matter, too.

Interruption protection: Are there times when team members are protected from interruptions to support focused work? Or is constant availability the expectation? Some roles require constant availability, but even small pockets of protected time can help.

Information flow management: How much information are team members expected to process? How is it organized? Is there a signal among the noise, or does everything come in at the same priority? Streamlined, well-organized information systems reduce cognitive load.

Clear protocols: When people know what to do in common situations, they don't have to figure it out each time. Good protocols are cognitive scaffolding. They support quick, confident action without requiring extensive mental processing.

Decision authority: When team members have clear authority to make certain decisions, they spend less energy wondering whether they're allowed to act or if they need approval. Clarity about decision rights reduces cognitive friction.

Adequate staffing: When there are enough people to handle the work, each person's cognitive load is manageable. When staffing is inadequate, everyone is constantly overwhelmed. This seems obvious, but the cognitive cost of chronic understaffing is often underestimated.

Technology that helps: Good technology reduces cognitive load by handling routine tasks, providing easy access to information, and supporting workflow. Bad technology increases cognitive load by being confusing, unreliable, or requiring constant attention. Every technology choice is also a cognitive choice.

MENTAL CLARITY AND SERVICE QUALITY

The connection is direct. When David's mind went blank on a simple restaurant recommendation, he wasn't providing excellent service. He wasn't even providing average service. He was struggling to provide basic service because his cognitive capacity was exhausted.

Multiply that moment across every team member, every shift, every day. The cumulative effect of cognitive overload is an organization that's always operating below its capability, not because people don't care or aren't trained, but because their brains aren't sufficiently resourced to access what they know and apply it effectively.

The guest doesn't experience "cognitive overload." They experience someone who seems distracted, who doesn't remember what they asked for, who makes mistakes, who doesn't anticipate their needs, who seems to be somewhere else even while standing right in front of them.

Mental wellness isn't separate from service quality. It's the operating system that makes quality possible.

When David has the capacity to actually think, he doesn't just know a good Italian restaurant. He remembers that this guest mentioned a gluten allergy at check-in and recommends a place with great gluten-free options. He notices that she seems stressed and offers to make the reservation for her. He creates a moment of genuine helpfulness instead of just processing a transaction.

That's the difference mental capacity makes. It's available when we take cognitive wellness as seriously as we take training, standards, and service protocols.

CHAPTER 8

EMOTIONAL—THE HEART THAT KEEPS GIVING

Henry has been at this property for seven years.

He started in his late twenties as a concierge, drawn to the role because he genuinely loved helping people. There was something deeply satisfying about solving problems, making connections, and turning someone's frustrating situation into a story they'd tell friends about later. He was good at it. Guests requested him by name. Management noticed. He built a reputation for being the person who could handle anything with grace.

A year ago, he was moved to the front desk because of a staffing shortage, and management knew he would be an asset there. Less emotionally demanding. Fewer miracles required. Tonight, the concierge has gone home, and he's the one a guest finds.

She's in Lululemon, hair in a messy bun, and gripping her phone like a lifeline. Henry can see a photo on the locked screen: a little girl in a leotard. He's seen this mom at the lobby coffee bar a couple of times since they checked in. Her eyes are tired. She's overcaffeinated, but it's not doing the job.

She launches in without greeting. Her daughter's ballet recital is tomorrow. They flew in specifically for this event. Tonight, while laying out the costume, she noticed a hole in the leotard. A small tear along the seam, but it's only going to get worse under stage lights. Her daughter is upstairs crying. The recital is at 10 a.m. Nothing will be open. She needs a miracle.

Seven years ago, Henry would have immediately started problem-solving. What does she need? How can I help? What creative solution might this require?

Tonight, he feels something closer to dread.

The thought comes before he can stop it: *Concierge has gone home. This isn't my job anymore.* He knows taking care of this in the morning would be too late, but he considers saying it anyway.

He catches the thought and feels a wave of shame. When did he become this person?

He takes a breath. He puts on the face.

"I'm going to take care of this. What size does your daughter wear?"

He does the work. He makes calls, finds a dancewear store that will open early, and arranges transportation. He's done versions of this a hundred times.

The next day, he walks in, his manager says, "Nice work," and hands him a note from the woman expressing her gratitude for his help. An hour into his shift, she shows up at the desk. She's transformed: makeup done, hair fixed, daughter bouncing next to her. The mom laughs, almost disbelieving. "How did you even … I don't … thank you. The recital was a huge success."

On the drive home, he replayed the moment. The mom's face. The daughter full of renewed excitement. For the first time in months, he felt a flicker of something he thought he'd lost. It wasn't enough to erase the exhaustion. But it was something.

THE EMOTIONAL DIMENSION OF SERVICE

Hospitality is emotional labor. Not emotional labor in the casual sense of "work that's emotionally difficult," but emotional labor in the precise sense: work that requires managing your emotions as part of the job.

Every service interaction involves an emotional exchange. Guests arrive carrying their own emotional states: excitement, frustration, anxiety, grief, joy, and exhaustion. Your job, in part, is to receive those emotions appropriately, regulate your own emotional response, and project the emotional tone the situation requires.

This is skilled work. It's also expensive work. Unlike physical labor, where we can see someone getting tired and offer them a break, emotional labor is invisible. Henry looks fine. He's doing his job. No one can see that his emotional tank is nearly empty.

Emotional wellness is having enough capacity to acknowledge, process, and respond to emotions (yours and others') without being overwhelmed. It's the difference between choosing to be warm and having to force warmth between genuine empathy and performed empathy.

When emotional capacity is full, hospitality work feels natural. You have room to receive what guests bring. You have flexibility in how you respond. You recover from difficult interactions without carrying them into the next.

When emotional capacity is depleted, everything becomes heavier. You start protecting yourself from emotional engagement because you don't have enough to give. The warmth that used to flow naturally has to be manufactured. The gap between what you're feeling and what you're projecting becomes a constant drain.

DEEP ACTING VS. SURFACE ACTING

Arlie Hochschild, who coined the term *emotional labor* in her book *The Managed Heart*, distinguishes between two approaches: deep acting and surface acting.[1]

Surface acting is changing your external expression without changing your internal state. You're feeling irritated, but you paste on a smile. You're feeling disconnected, but you use warm words. There's a gap between inside and outside, and managing that gap takes constant effort.

Surface acting is exhausting and unsustainable. It's what people mean when they say they feel like they're "being fake" at work. The effort to maintain performance creates its own drain. Guests often sense the gap, even when they can't name it. Something feels off. The warmth doesn't quite reach the eyes.

Deep acting is actually shifting your internal state to match what the situation requires. Instead of pretending you're not irritated, you find a way to genuinely let go of the irritation. Instead of performing empathy, you access actual empathy. The inside and the outside align because you've done internal work to create that alignment.

Deep acting is more sustainable and more effective. When the warmth is real, guests feel it. When the empathy is genuine, it creates actual connection. The authenticity shows.

But deep acting requires something that surface acting doesn't: emotional capacity. You need internal resources to do the work of shifting your state. When you're depleted, deep acting becomes impossible. You don't have the reserves to genuinely transform your emotional experience. Surface acting becomes the only option, and the gap between inside and outside widens.

This is what's happening to Henry. He used to have enough emotional capacity to do deep acting, to genuinely connect with guests' distress, to feel real satisfaction in solving their problems, to authentically care about ballet costumes and crying children. Now he's running on surface acting, and he can feel the difference.

Randy Remembers: Deep Acting in Practice

At one point Randy was dealing with his daughter being bullied in school, while his parents across the country were having health issues.

His ritual was that before he got out of his car, he would say to himself, "All of this will be here when I get off work and back to the car. I'll deal with it then. For now, I get to play and make magic for our guests. Go have fun!"

As he walked from his car to the resort, he would take some deep breaths and walk slowly. When he crossed the street and saw the resort, he would smile and think about how lucky he was to be working here.

On one day when he was having a particularly tough morning, he did his ritual, went to work, and about two hours into his shift, a guest looked at him, smiled, and said, "Wow! You have the most amazing energy around you." Randy smiled back and asked if he could give her a hug. She said "yes," and he gave her a friendly embrace.

Deep acting doesn't mean ignoring emotional stressors. You acknowledge the stress, then let it go for now so you can shift your internal state to match what the situation requires.

COMPASSION FATIGUE

There's a name for what happens when people who care for others run out of emotional capacity: compassion fatigue.

Originally identified in healthcare workers, compassion fatigue is now recognized across helping professions, including hospitality. It's the emotional and physical exhaustion that comes from prolonged exposure to others' suffering or stress, combined with the demands of responding with care.

Signs of compassion fatigue include:

Reduced empathy is often the first sign. The natural response to care about others' distress becomes muted or absent. You hear about problems and feel nothing or feel annoyed rather than concerned.

There's often **emotional numbing**, too. To protect yourself from overwhelm, you stop feeling much of anything. The world becomes flat. Things that used to move you don't anymore.

Cynicism creeps in. Negativity about guests, the job, and humanity in general appears. You form the belief that people are demanding, unreasonable, and never satisfied.

You might notice **detachment**, withdrawing from emotional engagement with work and, sometimes, from personal relationships, too, where you're going through the motions without presence.

Intrusive thoughts are common. You replay difficult interactions, worry about situations that have already been resolved, or have dreams about work problems.

Physical symptoms show up, too: exhaustion that sleep doesn't help with, headaches, digestive issues, and more frequent illness.

And eventually, **decreased job satisfaction.** Work that used to be fulfilling feels empty. The sense of meaning drains away.

Compassion fatigue isn't weakness. It's what happens when emotional output exceeds emotional input for too long. It's the entirely predictable result of caring work without adequate support for the carers. A car won't run on an empty tank.

Henry is not bad at his job. He's depleted. The solution isn't to work harder or care more. It's to address the underlying depletion so that caring becomes possible again.

THE EMOTIONAL TOLL

Some drains are inherent to service work. Others are optional, created by culture, systems, or personal patterns. Consider that most of us were raised with a skewed sense of emotions. We live in a society of emotional anorexia where we're taught to stuff or ignore our feelings. Men often express anger when they feel hurt or sad. Women may cry when they feel angry. Getting in touch with and enhancing your emotional self will vastly improve your customer service skills and emotional capacity.

Constant emotional reception: Every guest interaction involves receiving whatever emotional state the guest brings. Over a shift, that's dozens or hundreds of emotional exchanges. Even when individual interactions aren't difficult, the cumulative effect of constant reception can be draining.

Difficult interactions without recovery: A truly difficult interaction (an angry guest, an unreasonable demand, verbal abuse, emotional manipulation) requires significant emotional processing. When these happen, and there's no time or space to recover before the next interaction, the emotional wound stays open and can fester.

Lack of emotional validation: When your emotional experience isn't acknowledged or is dismissed ("Don't take it personally," "Just shake it off," "It's part of the job"), the emotions don't process. They accumulate. Having space to say, "That was really hard," and having someone respond with "Yes, it was," makes an enormous difference.

Surface acting demands: When the culture requires constant positivity regardless of how you feel, the gap between inside and outside becomes chronic. Every shift becomes an extended performance, and the performance is exhausting.

Absorbing rather than witnessing: There's a difference between witnessing someone's distress (being present to it without taking it on) and absorbing it (making it your own). Service workers often absorb emotions rather than just witness them. The guest's anxiety becomes your anxiety. Their frustration becomes your frustration. This magnifies the emotional cost.

Poor boundaries: When you don't have clear lines between your emotional responsibility and others', everything becomes yours to carry. The guest's problem becomes your problem in a way that exceeds what's actually helpful.

Life stress compounding work stress: Emotional capacity is one resource pool. When personal life is emotionally demanding (relationship struggles, family illness, financial stress, grief), there's less available for work. When work is emotionally demanding, there's less available for personal life. The two can spiral together.

REFILLING THE TANK

Recovery happens when emotional input exceeds emotional output for long enough to restore the balance. Think of it like a bank balance. It's important to make enough deposits to handle what you withdraw. Taking out more than you have available incurs interest payments, and over time, this can leave you feeling bankrupt.

Processing time: Emotions need to be felt and processed, not stuffed down or pushed through. Time to reflect on difficult interactions, to name what you felt, to let the feelings move through you rather than getting stuck. This can be private (journaling or thinking on a walk) or shared (debriefing with a trusted colleague or talking to a therapist).

Emotional validation: Having someone acknowledge your emotional experience without attempting to fix it or minimize it. "That sounds really frustrating," or "No wonder you're exhausted," or simply being heard by someone who understands. Validation doesn't change the circumstances, but it helps the emotions process.

Genuine connection: Not transactional interaction, but real human contact where you're seen and known. Time with friends and family who care about you as a person, not just what you can do for them. Relationships where you receive care as well as give it.

Experiences that generate positive emotion: Activities that fill you with joy, satisfaction, peace, excitement, and gratitude. Whatever those are for you, make sure they're part of your life regularly. Positive emotions aren't just pleasant. They're restorative.

Physical care: Emotional and physical capacity are interconnected. Sleep, nutrition, exercise, and rest all support emotional resilience. When the body is depleted, emotional resilience suffers.

The "best friend voice": The internal dialogue from chapter 4 matters enormously for emotional wellness. When your internal voice is critical and harsh, it's an ongoing emotional drain. When it's supportive and compassionate, it provides a baseline of emotional care that supports everything else.

Boundaries: Clear limits on what's yours to carry and what isn't. The ability to care about someone's problem without becoming responsible for solving everything. The capacity to say no when yes would cost too much. Good boundaries protect emotional capacity.

Professional support: Sometimes the accumulated emotional weight needs professional help to process. Therapy, counseling, and coaching aren't signs of failure. They're tools for maintaining the emotional wellness that demanding work requires. We're taught that asking for help is a weakness when, in fact, it's a strength.

PRACTICAL STRATEGIES FOR EMOTIONAL SUSTAINABILITY

The separation ritual: Create a practice that marks the boundary between work and not-work. It might be changing clothes, taking a specific route home, listening to particular music, or a few minutes of quiet in your car before you go in. The ritual signals to your brain that life situations stay here; I'm entering a different space now.

The debrief: After difficult shifts or interactions, process them. This might be talking with a colleague ("That check-in was intense, wasn't it?") or writing a few sentences in a journal. Randy recalls a colleague who was one of the most relaxed and friendliest people at the resort. During breaks, he would see her sitting at a table, writing. Once, he asked her what she was writing. She looked up and said, "I'm writing in my journal. It helps calm me." In the debrief, you may just sit quietly and let yourself feel what you feel. Don't skip straight from hard work to "everything is fine."

Identify your triggers: We all have situations that set us off emotionally, often rooted in past experiences. Knowing your triggers and recognizing when they're activated makes the reaction more manageable. You're not eliminating the response. You're catching it earlier. This is where the pause really comes in handy.

The witness stance: Practice witnessing others' emotions without absorbing them. You can be fully present to someone's distress while maintaining awareness that it's their distress, not yours. This isn't cold or detached. It's sustainable compassion. You're standing beside them, not merging with them.

The recovery bookmark: When something emotionally intense happens during a shift, and you don't have time to process it, consciously mark it: "I'm going to set this aside for now and come back to it." This is different from pushing it away. You're acknowledging it needs attention and committing to giving it that attention later.

The support network: Identify people you can talk to honestly about the emotional demands of your work: colleagues who understand, friends who listen, or family members who care. Isolation amplifies depletion. Connection supports recovery.

The joy investment: Regularly invest in experiences that generate positive emotion. Less passive consumption (watching TV, scrolling), more active engagement with things that bring you alive. Make this non-negotiable, especially when work is emotionally demanding. One of Randy's favorite sayings is, "Joy is not a reward, it's a resource."

The self-compassion practice: When you notice compassion fatigue symptoms, meet them with compassion rather than judgment. You're not broken or failing. You're depleted. You need care, not criticism. What would you say to a colleague experiencing what you're experiencing? Say that to yourself.

ORGANIZATIONAL SUPPORT FOR EMOTIONAL WELLNESS

Individual practices matter, but organizational culture matters more. Some environments make emotional wellness possible. Others make it nearly impossible.

Cultures that acknowledge emotional labor: Organizations that recognize service work as emotionally demanding, that name it, and factor it into workload and scheduling have better outcomes than organizations that treat emotional labor as invisible and expect infinite emotional availability.

Space for processing: Companies that allow time to recover after difficult interactions, give permission to step away briefly when needed, and debrief practices built into the workday are more successful than environments where it's straight from one interaction to the next, with no recovery.

Validation structures: Managers who check in about emotional experience, not just task completion, and foster peer support systems and team cultures where it's okay to say, "That was hard," tend to run more smoothly than environments where emotional struggle is seen as weakness to be hidden.

Protection from abuse: Create clear policies that prohibit guest abuse of team members and reinforce that managers are to back up their people, which fosters cultures that are more successful than cultures where "the customer is always right" extends to tolerating mistreatment.

Access to support: Provide an employee assistance program, mental health resources, and paths to professional support without stigma. Recognize that emotional well-being may sometimes require professional intervention.

Leaders who want emotionally resilient teams need to examine whether their practices support or undermine that resilience. It's not enough to tell people to take care of themselves while creating conditions that make self-care difficult.

EMOTIONAL WELLNESS AND SERVICE QUALITY

When Henry had emotional capacity, his service had a quality that's hard to name but easy to feel. Guests experienced someone who genuinely cared, who took real pleasure in solving their problems, and who was fully present to their experience. That quality is what creates memorable service, what generates the stories guests tell about a property, and what builds loyalty that transcends price and convenience.

When Henry is depleted, the technical service might be identical. He still solves the ballet costume problem. He still makes the calls, arranges the transportation, and delivers the result. But something is missing. The mother gets her daughter's costume, but she doesn't experience genuine care from another human being. She gets competence without warmth, resolution without connection.

This is the cost of emotional depletion that doesn't show up on any metric. The solved problems get counted, but the emotional cost is missed.

Your team's emotional wellness isn't a personal matter separate from their professional performance. It's the source of the quality that makes service memorable. When that source is depleted, all the training and standards in the world won't produce what emotionally healthy people produce naturally.

Don't treat Henry as a project to fix. He's a signal. Something about the demands on him has exceeded what's sustainable. Either those demands need to change, his resources need to increase, or both. Because the hospitality industry needs people like Henry, people who genuinely care about ballet costumes and crying children, and those people will stay and stay healthy, only if we create conditions where caring is sustainable.

CHAPTER 9

SPIRITUAL—FINDING MEANING IN THE WORK

Julia has been a catering manager for eight years.

She started as a server, working banquets during college. She remembers standing in an empty ballroom at nine o'clock in the morning, tables bare, and then standing in the same room at seven in the evening, transformed. Two hundred people are celebrating. She made that happen. She used to tell people she helped make memories. She meant it.

She moved up quickly. Server to captain to assistant manager to manager. She has a reputation for flawless execution. Her events run smoothly. Her team respects her. The numbers are good.

But something has shifted, and she's having trouble naming what it is.

Last Saturday, she managed a wedding reception for 200 guests. The couple's first dance was "Bless the Broken Road." Ten years ago, that song would have wrecked her. She used to believe every word of it. Saturday, she heard the opening notes and felt nothing. Just checked that the spotlight operator was in position.

At the end of the night, the bride found her to say thank you. Julia said all the right words. She's said them so many times they don't mean anything anymore. "Making memories" sounds like a line from a brochure now.

She used to go home full after nights like this. Now she just goes home.

Julia hasn't burned out in the traditional sense. She's not exhausted, overwhelmed, or ready to quit. She has something harder to fix: She's lost the thread. The thing that made this career meaningful has gone quiet, and she doesn't know how to find it again.

THE DIMENSION WE DON'T TALK ABOUT

Physical wellness, mental clarity, and emotional capacity: These are concepts most workplaces at least acknowledge, even if they don't support them well. But spiritual wellness? That's where people get uncomfortable.

Let's be clear about what we mean. Spiritual wellness is about meaning, purpose, and connection to something larger than yourself and your immediate concerns. Where that connection comes from varies enormously from person to person. Religious faith, humanistic values, commitment to craft, love of community, or a sense of a calling to serve others.

These sources of meaning often overlap and blend in ways unique to each individual. What matters isn't the source. It's whether you have access to a felt sense that your work connects to something bigger than you, that matters to you.

Research by psychologist Amy Wrzesniewski has shown that people who view their work as a calling rather than just a job report higher satisfaction and better performance, regardless of the work itself.[1]

It's the dimension of human experience that asks: Why does this matter? What's the point? How does my work connect to something beyond a paycheck and a performance review?

Every human being has this dimension. We're meaning-making creatures. Some people attempt to fill this need with power or money, but it never quite works. There's always a hunger for more, a hole that never gets filled. We want to feel that our efforts contribute to something, that our presence makes a difference, that our work has significance beyond its transactional value.

When this dimension is resourced, work has an aliveness. Even difficult days feel worth it because they connect to something you care about. The effort makes sense. The sacrifice has a reason.

When this dimension is depleted, work becomes hollow. You might still be competent. You might still hit your numbers. But the spark is gone. You're going through motions that used to mean something, and you're not sure why you're still going through them.

Julia's situation is one of spiritual depletion. Her body is fine. Her mind is sharp. Her emotional capacity is adequate. But the meaning has drained out, and without meaning, everything else feels pointless.

THE HOSPITALITY CRISIS OF MEANING

Hospitality work is particularly vulnerable to spiritual depletion because its meaning depends so much on connection.

At its best, hospitality is one of the most rewarding forms of work. You spend your days making people's experiences better. You help celebrate their milestones, ease their travels, and support them through difficult times. You create moments that matter. Few careers offer such direct access to making a difference in people's lives.

But that meaning depends on actually experiencing the connection. When work becomes transactional, when guests become room numbers, covers, and occupancy percentages, the meaning evaporates. The technical work might be identical, but the experience of doing it is completely different.

This is what happens to so many hospitality professionals. They enter the industry because they genuinely enjoy caring for people. Over time, the systems, pressures, and sheer volume of interactions transform that personal calling into an industrial process. They're still technically taking care of people. But they've stopped experiencing it that way.

The industry measures everything by occupancy rates, customer satisfaction scores, service speed, and retention numbers. However, none of these metrics captures whether a catering manager still feels the magic of a wedding or whether she's just executing a timeline. And yet, this unmeasured dimension might matter more than anything else to the above-mentioned metrics. Because when the meaning goes, so does the quality that makes hospitality memorable. You might still deliver competent service, but you won't deliver the kind of service that transforms a stay into a story, a meal into a memory, an event into a milestone.

WHAT SPIRITUAL DEPLETION LOOKS LIKE

Julia's experience, competent execution without felt meaning, is one manifestation. There are others.

Cynicism about the work itself: You have the belief that hospitality is "just" serving people, "just" making beds, "just" running events. The word *just* is diagnostic. It minimizes significance. It drains meaning from work that, experienced fully, has profound significance.

Disconnection from impact: You're unable to see or feel the difference your work makes. The bride's tears don't register. The guest's gratitude doesn't register emotionally. The evidence of impact is right there, but it doesn't penetrate.

Values misalignment: The organization's actual values (as demonstrated by behavior, not mission statements) conflict with your own. You're asked to prioritize things you don't believe matter or deprioritize things you know do matter.

Existential questioning: This is not the healthy kind of questioning that leads to growth, but the draining kind: *What's the point? Why am I doing this? Does any of this matter?* These questions without satisfying answers are spiritually expensive.

Isolation: You're feeling alone in your work and disconnected from others who share your purpose. You have the sense that you're a solo operator rather than part of something collective.

Going through motions: This is the autopilot experience of showing up, doing the tasks, going home, and repeating. The external behavior remains unchanged while the internal experience empties.

Envy of other paths: You frequently fantasize about different careers that seem more meaningful. The grass-is-greener pattern suggests the meaning problem is about the work rather than about how you're relating to it.

WHAT DRAINS THE SPIRITUAL DIMENSION

Some drains are inherent to how modern work is structured. Others are specific to hospitality. Some are organizational. Some are personal.

Transactional framing: When the organization treats guests as revenue sources rather than people to serve, team members are viewed as labor costs rather than humans with contributions to make, and everything is reduced to transactions, meaning suffocates.

Volume overwhelming connection: When there are so many guests, so many events, and so many interactions, genuine connection becomes impossible. You simply don't have the bandwidth to see each person as a person. They become a blur.

Metrics that miss meaning: When you're measured on speed, efficiency, and error rates, those become what matters.

The unmeasured dimensions (connection, care, meaning) get squeezed out because they don't count in any official way.

Being treated as interchangeable: When the organization signals that you're a replaceable unit, that your individual presence doesn't matter, or that anyone could do what you do, this is spiritually corrosive. Meaning requires mattering, and mattering requires being seen as a particular person, not a generic function.

Personal disconnection from purpose: Sometimes the drain is internal. You've lost touch with why you chose this work. The original motivation has faded. You're continuing out of momentum rather than meaning.

WHAT BUILDS THE SPIRITUAL DIMENSION

Meaning isn't something you find once and keep forever. It requires ongoing cultivation. Like a garden, it needs tending.

Making impact visible: Create opportunities to actually see the difference your work makes. Read guest feedback, hear the stories of problems solved, and witness celebrations you made possible. All of these are evidence of impact, which is often there but goes unseen. Making it visible reconnects work to meaning.

Values alignment: Work in organizations whose actual values (not marketing messages, but real operating values) align with your own, and know that what the organization cares about is what you care about. When these values align, work becomes an expression of who you are rather than a role you perform.

Connection to something larger: Hospitality, at its essence, is about human care. It's one of the oldest and most fundamental forms of work: welcoming strangers, providing sustenance and shelter, creating space for human experience. Connecting your daily tasks to this larger tradition and purpose can restore meaning that narrow job descriptions obscure.

The "We Over Me" philosophy: You feel like you're part of a team working toward a shared purpose, knowing that your contribution combines with others' to create something no one could create alone. This creates a shift from being an isolated individual performer to a member of a collective with a mission. This is profoundly meaningful for most people. (We'll explore this fully in Part Five.)

Recognition of human significance: Having your particular contribution seen and valued. Not generic praise, but specific acknowledgment of what you, uniquely, bring. Being treated as a person who matters, not a function to be performed.

Rituals of meaning: Create practices that reconnect you to purpose. For some, this might be meditation or prayer. For others, it might be reading feedback at the start of a shift, a team huddle that reinforces shared purpose, or a personal practice of noticing moments that mattered. Regular rituals counter the drift toward meaninglessness.

Teaching and mentoring: Share what you know with new hires, helping them develop and contributing to their growth. Teaching forces you to articulate why things matter, which often reconnects you to your own sense of meaning. Seeing others grow because of your contribution is inherently meaningful.

Creative engagement: Find ways to bring creativity to your work and solve problems in new ways. Creativity is an expression of agency and significance. When you're just executing someone else's plan, meaning suffers. When you're contributing your own ideas and approaches, meaning increases.

THE "ONE LIGHT, MANY LAMPSHADES" PRINCIPLE

The spiritual dimension doesn't require any particular framework to flourish.

Randy often says there's one light but many lampshades. Whatever framework gives your work meaning is valid. For some people, it's explicitly religious: Their work is an expression of faith, a form of service to God, a living out of spiritual values. Others ground it in humanism, caring about human flourishing and seeing hospitality as a way to contribute to it. Some find it in beauty, taking real meaning from creating excellence in service. And for others, it's relational: The connections with guests and colleagues are what matter.

None of these frameworks is better than another. What matters is having a framework, a way of understanding why your work matters that connects your daily tasks to something you care about.

The problem isn't that people lack spiritual frameworks. It's that the frameworks get buried under pressure, volume, and organizational systems that treat work purely as a transaction.

The spiritual dimension is still there. It's just been neglected until it went quiet.

Part of the work of spiritual wellness is excavating your own framework. *What made you choose this work? What do you actually care about? When has this work felt most meaningful, and what was present then that might be missing now?* These aren't abstract philosophical questions. They're practical questions about sustainability and quality.

PRACTICAL STRATEGIES FOR SPIRITUAL WELLNESS

Meaning audit: Periodically ask yourself, *Where is meaning present in my work? Where is it absent? What's draining it? What might restore it?* This isn't navel-gazing. It's the maintenance of your most important professional resource.

Impact collection: Actively collect evidence of your impact. Save positive feedback. Take note of problems you solved and guests you helped. Create a folder (physical or digital) of moments that mattered. When meaning runs low, return to this evidence.

Larger frame: Regularly zoom out from daily tasks to the larger purpose they serve. The bed you're making is where someone will rest after a long day. The event you're catering is someone's celebration of something important. The problem you're solving is removing stress from someone's experience. The frame matters.

Community of purpose: Cultivate relationships with people who share your sense of why this work matters. The cynics will always be present. Seek out the people who still believe, who still care, who still find meaning. Their energy is contagious, but so is the energy of chronic cynicism. Choose your community carefully.

Gratitude practice: Regularly notice what you're grateful for in your work (and in your life). This is not forced positivity, but genuine recognition of what's good. The people you work with. The moments that go well. The environment you're part of. Gratitude and meaning are closely connected. Cultivating one tends to strengthen the other.

ORGANIZATIONAL SUPPORT FOR SPIRITUAL WELLNESS

Individual practices help, but organizational culture determines whether meaning flourishes or withers.

Mission that's lived, not laminated: Every organization has a mission statement. Very few have missions that actually guide decisions and shape behavior. When the mission is real, when it's referenced in meetings, when decisions are tested against it, when leaders actually believe it, that's fertile ground for spiritual wellness. When the mission is marketing, everyone knows it, and the cynicism spreads.

Stories, not just statistics: Organizations that regularly share stories of impact (guests helped, problems solved, lives touched) feed the spiritual dimension. Organizations that only share numbers starve it. Both matter, but numbers alone don't move people.

Recognition of individual contribution: Organizations need systems that see and acknowledge what each person brings. These are not generic employee-of-the-month programs, but specific recognition that says: This is what you did, this is why it mattered, this is how it contributed to our purpose.

Voice and agency: People need environments where they have input, their ideas are heard, and they have some control over how work gets done. Meaning requires agency. Pure compliance is spiritually deadening.

Leaders who embody meaning: This requires managers and executives who visibly connect to purpose, communicate why the work matters, and treat the mission as real. Leadership is modeling. When leaders are transactional and cynical, that spreads. When they're genuinely connected to purpose, that spreads too.

SPIRITUAL WELLNESS AND SERVICE QUALITY

Julia, managing last Saturday's wedding, executed flawlessly. The bride and groom will probably never know that their catering manager felt nothing. The timeline was perfect. The food was excellent. The evening flowed smoothly.

But something was missing, and on some level, everyone felt it.

The couple received competent service. They didn't receive the kind of care that makes people feel held on their important days. They didn't experience someone who saw their wedding as sacred, as a moment that mattered, as something worth bringing her full presence to.

This is the spiritual dimension's contribution to service quality. It's not about efficiency, accuracy, or consistency. It's about presence, care, and the felt sense that the person serving you believes your experience matters.

When that dimension is alive, service has a quality that's hard to define but easy to feel. Guests sense they're in the presence of people who care about what they're doing, believe in the work, and bring something of themselves to every interaction.

When that dimension is dead, service becomes mechanical. It's technically correct but spiritually empty. Guests receive what they asked for but not what they came for, which is, at bottom, to feel that they matter.

The hospitality industry is in the business of making people feel they matter. That only happens when the people delivering the hospitality feel that they matter, too, that their work matters, and that the person in front of them matters.

That's the spiritual dimension. It's not optional. It's central to everything.

THE TRANSITION TO "WE"

Throughout Part Three, we've focused on individual dimensions: your physical wellness, mental clarity, emotional capacity, and spiritual meaning. And individual attention to these dimensions is essential.

When individuals who've done this work come together, they create something none of them could create alone.

Part Four will address what organizations and leaders can do differently to create environments where individual wellness becomes possible. Part Five will explore what happens when healthy individuals come together as teams with collective confidence and shared purpose.

Because the deepest meaning in hospitality isn't found alone; it's found in the experience of being part of something, of "We Over Me," of a collective effort toward shared purpose.

Julia's spiritual depletion isn't just about her individual relationship to meaning. It's also about what's missing in her team, her organization, and her connection to something larger than her individual performance.

Restoring her spark might require individual work. But it might also require finding her way back into genuine community with others who share her purpose.

That's where we're heading next.

PART FOUR

BUILDING CULTURES WHERE WORTH FLOURISHES

Everything we've explored so far, the internal voice, the energy ball, and the four dimensions of wellness, happens within individuals. But individuals don't operate in isolation. They work within systems, cultures, and environments that either support or undermine their capacity to thrive.

You can do all the personal work in the world, develop your "best friend voice," manage your energy, and tend to your physical, mental, emotional, and spiritual wellness, but still find yourself depleted if you're working in an environment that constantly drains what you're striving to build.

This is where leadership and organizational culture become essential.

Part Four shifts our focus from what individuals need to do for themselves to what organizations and leaders need to do differently. This is not instead of individual work, but in addition to it. Both are necessary. Neither alone is sufficient.

We'll examine the trap of mechanical service and why it persists despite its obvious limitations. We'll explore psychological safety and why it's the foundation for everything else. We'll look at what leadership actually looks like when the goal is building cultures where worth flourishes.

CHAPTER 10

BREAKING THE MECHANICAL SERVICE TRAP

There's a reason the "smile harder" approach persists despite everything we've said about its limitations.

It's measurable. It's trainable. It's controllable.

You can write a script. People can be taught to follow it. Compliance is observable, and deviations are correctable. The result is consistency across locations, shifts, and team members, all of it captured in a manual you can hand to the next hire and call your service standard.

This is enormously appealing to organizations. The messiness of human beings, with their varying energy levels and internal voices, emotional states, and spiritual needs, is replaced by a system. The unpredictability of genuine human connection is replaced by the reliable execution of defined behaviors.

The problem, of course, is that it doesn't actually work. Not in the way that matters.

Mechanical service produces mechanical experiences. Guests receive the scripted words, the trained behaviors, and the standardized interactions. They don't receive what they actually came for: a genuine sense of being welcomed, cared for, and valued by another human being.

But breaking free from mechanical service is harder than it sounds. It requires organizations to trust their people more, control less, and accept a level of variability that makes many leaders deeply uncomfortable.

WHY MECHANICAL SERVICE FEELS SAFE

Let's acknowledge what mechanical service offers because understanding the appeal is essential to moving beyond it.

Consistency: Every guest receives the same experience. No one gets the tired team member having a bad day. No one gets the brilliant improvisation that can't be replicated. Everything is standardized, predictable, and reliable.

Scalability: The approach works across hundreds or thousands of employees and dozens of locations. You don't need to develop each person's unique capacity for connection. You just need to train them on the script.

Measurability: You can observe compliance. Did they say the greeting? Did they offer the upsell? Did they use the guest's name? These are binary questions with clear answers. Mystery shoppers can evaluate. Managers can correct.

Risk reduction: When people improvise, they sometimes do so poorly, saying the wrong thing or making promises they shouldn't. They create liability. Scripts reduce this risk by limiting what people are authorized to say and do.

Speed of onboarding: New team members become "trained" quickly. They learn the script, follow the script, and are operational. You don't have to wait for them to develop judgment, intuition, or genuine connection skills.

These benefits are real. Organizations that adopt mechanical service aren't all cold and heartless. They're responding to genuine challenges of scale, consistency, and control.

The question is: What are they giving up? Is the trade-off worth it?

WHAT MECHANICAL SERVICE ACTUALLY COSTS

The costs are substantial, but they're often invisible or attributed to other causes.

Ceiling on experience quality: Mechanical service has a ceiling. It produces adequate experiences but rarely exceptional ones. The moments guests remember and tell stories about almost always involve something that went beyond the script or someone who responded to them as a particular person rather than a generic guest.

Employee disengagement: People who are reduced to script-followers tend to disengage. The work becomes monotonous. There's no room for creativity or judgment. The sense of meaning drains away because you're not really doing anything; you're just executing someone else's plan. Turnover increases. The people who stay often check out mentally.

Inability to handle the unexpected: Scripts work for predictable situations. Real service involves constant unpredictability: unusual requests, emotional guests, and situations the manual didn't anticipate. Script-trained employees often freeze or defer when they encounter something off-script, precisely when a flexible human response is most needed.

Guest perception of inauthenticity: Guests aren't fooled. They can tell the difference between someone who genuinely cares and someone who's reading from a playbook. The scripted warmth often feels hollow. "Is there anything else I can help you with today?" comes across differently when it's clearly a required phrase versus a genuine offer.

Loss of competitive advantage: When everyone follows similar scripts, the service becomes indistinguishable. There's nothing memorable, nothing differentiated, and nothing that creates loyalty beyond price and convenience.

Attraction and retention problems: The best hospitality professionals, the ones who genuinely love serving people and bring creativity and heart to the work, don't want to be script-followers. They go elsewhere, leaving organizations with team members who are willing to trade autonomy for security but don't bring the spark that makes service special.

THE EITHER/OR TRAP

Here's where many organizations get stuck: They believe the choice is between mechanical consistency and chaotic inconsistency. Either you control everything through scripts and standards, or you let everyone do whatever they want and hope for the best.

But those aren't the only two options.

The alternative to mechanical service isn't no standards. It's *different* standards. Shifting from compliance-based standards (Did you follow the script?) to outcome-based standards (Did the guest feel genuinely cared for?). Develop people's capacity for judgment rather than removing the need for judgment. Create frameworks that guide without constraining.

Think about the difference between a recipe and a cooking philosophy.

A recipe tells you exactly what to do: these ingredients, these quantities, these steps, this timing. Follow it precisely, and you'll get a predictable result. This is mechanical service.

A cooking philosophy teaches you principles: balance flavors, use fresh ingredients, taste as you go, and adjust for your particular circumstances. Armed with these principles, you can create countless dishes, adapting to what's available, what your guests prefer, and what the moment calls for. This is what we're after.

Both produce food. But one produces the same dish every time, while the other produces an infinite variety of dishes that all share an underlying quality.

WHAT FRAMEWORKS LOOK LIKE

Moving beyond mechanical service requires replacing scripts with frameworks.

A script says: "Welcome to [Property Name]. My name is [Your Name]. How may I assist you today?"

A framework says: "Make guests feel personally welcomed. Use your own words. Make eye contact. Convey that you're genuinely glad they're here and ready to help."

The outcome is the same: Guests feel welcomed. But the path to that outcome honors the humanity of the team member. They get to be themselves. They bring their own warmth, style, and authentic presence.

A script says: "I apologize for the inconvenience. Let me see what I can do to resolve this for you."

A framework says, "When something goes wrong, acknowledge it genuinely. Don't be defensive. Focus on making it right. You have the authority to [specific empowerments]. Use your judgment about what would make this guest feel whole."

Again, it's the same outcome: The guest with a problem feels heard and helped. But the team member operates from understanding and judgment, not rote recitation.

Frameworks require more from team members. They require understanding the "why," not just the "what." They require judgment in applying principles to specific situations. They require genuine presence rather than performance.

This is exactly why they produce better results. When you have to understand rather than just comply, you're engaged.

When you have to exercise judgment, you're present. When you get to be yourself, the authenticity shows.

THE TRUST PROBLEM

The reason organizations resist this shift is a lack of trust.

Scripts exist because organizations don't trust their people to make good decisions. And honestly? That distrust isn't always unfounded. Some people, given autonomy, will make poor choices. Some will say inappropriate things. Some will give away too much. Some will create problems that scripts would have prevented.

Distrust creates an environment that drives away the trustworthy. People who are capable of good judgment don't want to work in environments that treat them like they have none. So, they leave, or they never apply in the first place. What remains is a workforce that increasingly *does* require scripts because the script-averse have gone elsewhere.

It's a self-fulfilling prophecy. Treat people as incapable of judgment, and eventually, you'll be left with people who are.

The alternative is to hire for judgment in the first place, then develop it further, to create environments where good judgment is expected, supported, and rewarded, and to accept that mistakes will happen and treat them as learning opportunities rather than proof that control is needed.

This requires courage. It requires accepting variability. It requires giving up the illusion of control that scripts provide.

Most of all, it requires genuinely believing that your people are capable of more than following directions.

BUILDING JUDGMENT

If the goal is judgment rather than compliance, how do you build it?

Hire for values and disposition, not just skills. People who genuinely care about guests and have an intuitive sense for what good service feels like are your foundation. You can teach skills. Teaching orientation is much harder.

Always explain the why. When team members understand why something matters, they engage differently than when they're just told what to do. The "why" creates the foundation for judgment. When they encounter a situation that the rules don't cover, understanding the underlying purpose helps them figure out what to do.

Stories matter more than standards. Stories of great service moments communicate what you're after in ways that rules don't. They show judgment in action. They create a felt sense of what excellence looks like. A library of stories, shared regularly, becomes a kind of distributed wisdom that guides decision-making.

Give people a safe space to practice. Judgment develops through exercise. Give people opportunities to make decisions, handle situations, and figure things out. Debrief afterward: What did you consider? What would you do differently? This builds the muscle and also builds trust.

When someone misses the mark, coach rather than correct. When someone's judgment misses, the instinct is often to add a rule to prevent recurrence. Resist this. Instead, coach: Help them understand what they missed, what to consider next time, and how to think about similar situations. Rules accumulate until they become unmanageable. Developed judgment scales infinitely.

Celebrate good judgment. When someone handles a situation beautifully, using their judgment to create an outcome no script could have produced, make it visible. Celebrate it. Share the story. This signals what you value and encourages others to bring their judgment forward.

Tolerate imperfection. Some judgment calls will be wrong. If every mistake triggers a new rule, you'll quickly be back to scripts. Accept that imperfection is the cost of engagement, and it's worth paying.

FRAMEWORKS IN PRACTICE: AN EXAMPLE

Let's make this concrete. Consider how a hotel might handle the common situation of a guest requesting a late checkout.

Script approach: "Late checkout is available for a fee of $50. Check-out time is normally eleven a.m. Would you like me to add the late checkout to your reservation?"

This is clear, consistent, and completely devoid of judgment. Every guest gets the same answer regardless of circumstances.

Framework approach: "Our goal is to accommodate guests whenever possible while maintaining our ability to prepare rooms for arriving guests. Consider whether the hotel is full tonight. Is housekeeping able to handle a later turn? Is this guest celebrating something special or dealing with something difficult? Has this guest stayed with us before? Use your judgment to find a solution that serves both the guest and our operational needs. You have the authority to offer complimentary late checkout when circumstances warrant it."

This requires more. The team member has to actually think. They have to assess the situation. They might need a brief conversation to understand what's behind the request. They might offer something different to a first-time guest with a late flight than to a regular guest who's just asking out of convenience.

The outcomes will vary. Some guests will get a complimentary late checkout. Some will be offered it for a fee. Some will be declined. This variability is exactly what script-based organizations fear.

But look at what's gained: Team members are engaged rather than robotic. Guests are treated as individuals, not as transactions. Genuine problem-solving happens. Loyalty builds because guests experience being truly cared for, not processed.

When frontline team members lack the authority to exercise judgment, small rigidities cost more than they save. Randy experienced this as a guest: He stayed at a hotel for less than twelve hours, asked if the resort fee could be waived since he wouldn't use any amenities, and the desk clerk said no. She probably had no choice. But that $40 policy cost them a repeat guest. Randy has been back to that city a few times, but has stayed elsewhere each time.

The problem wasn't the clerk. The problem was a system that gave her no room to make a reasonable call.

THE TRANSITION CHALLENGE

Moving from mechanical service to framework-based service doesn't happen overnight. The transition creates real challenges.

For team members: Some will thrive with more autonomy. Others will flounder, having learned to rely on scripts. Expect a period of uncertainty as people develop the judgment muscles that haven't been exercised.

For managers: The job changes. There's less monitoring for compliance, more coaching for judgment, less correcting deviations, and more developing capacity. Some managers find this shift natural. Others struggle because their own skills were built in a compliance-focused environment.

For systems: Performance measurement has to evolve. You're not asking, "Did they follow the script?" You're asking, "Did they achieve the outcome? Did the guest feel cared for? Did they demonstrate good judgment?" This is harder to measure, but not impossible.

For culture: A culture of compliance has momentum. "We've always done it this way" is a powerful force. Leaders have to consistently reinforce the new approach, celebrate examples of good judgment, and resist the pull back toward scripts whenever something goes wrong.

The transition is worth it, but it's not free. Organizations that attempt it need to commit genuinely, not half-heartedly. Half-measures produce confusion: People don't know whether they're supposed to follow scripts or use judgment, so they do neither well.

WHAT STAYS CONTROLLED

Let's be clear: Moving beyond mechanical service doesn't mean abandoning all standards. Some things remain non-negotiable.

Safety: Anything involving guest or team member safety stays controlled. Protocols exist for reasons.

Legal and regulatory requirements: Compliance with laws and regulations isn't optional; it's required, regardless of judgment.

Brand fundamentals: Core elements that make your property or brand distinctive might be standardized: the signature scent, the specific amenity, or the defining ritual.

Critical processes: Some operational processes need consistency for quality control, such as how rooms are cleaned or how food is prepared. Where consistency is essential for quality or safety, maintain it.

The invitation isn't to abandon control entirely. It's about applying control thoughtfully: maintain it where it truly matters, but release it where human judgment produces better outcomes.

THE PAYOFF

Organizations that successfully move beyond mechanical service discover something remarkable: Their people become their competitive advantage.

When team members are engaged rather than compliant, they bring discretionary effort that scripts never access. They notice things. They anticipate needs. They create moments. They solve problems creatively. They build relationships with guests that drive loyalty.

When guests experience genuine human connection rather than processed interactions, they tell stories. They return. They recommend. They forgive imperfections because the relationship is real.

When the best hospitality professionals hear about an organization that trusts its people and creates space for genuine service, they want to work there. Talent attraction improves. Retention improves. The team gets stronger.

This is the payoff for breaking the mechanical service trap. It requires more trust, more development, more tolerance for variability. But what you get in return is something scripts never deliver: service that feels alive.

CHAPTER 11

PSYCHOLOGICAL SAFETY— THE SOIL WHERE WORTH GROWS

Marcus has been a server at a restaurant for three years. He's good at his job. He reads tables well, anticipates needs, and handles complaints with grace. His managers consider him reliable.

Last Tuesday, he noticed something that bothered him.

The boy is maybe eight or nine. Marcus notices him tugging at his collar. His face is flushed, but it's the way the color is creeping down his neck, blotchy and uneven, that catches Marcus's attention.

They've got him in one of the big corner booths with plenty of room to spread out. Smart parents. The restaurant is loud tonight; there's live music competing with conversation at every table. Mom and Dad are leaning in, talking about tomorrow's plans while stealing glances at the over-the-top decor like they can't believe they're actually here. They're not ignoring him. They're just having a moment. And the boy was fine a minute ago.

Marcus faces a decision. He rehearses it: "Hey, I just wanted to point out ..." But what if he's wrong? What if they already know? What if they complain?

He says nothing.

Twenty minutes later, the dad is rushing the boy out with the mom right behind. Marcus hears the word "ambulance" from the hostess stand.

The music is still playing. People at other tables are still eating. And Marcus is frozen, thinking: I could have said something.

The boy was fine, ultimately. But it was close.

Marcus replayed the moment for weeks afterward. Why didn't he speak up? He saw it. He knew something was wrong. He had the information that might have helped.

The answer was fear. Not of one thing, but of all of it: being wrong, overstepping, the complaint that might follow, and his manager's face if a guest said their server made them uncomfortable.

In the moment of decision, the risk of speaking up felt larger than the risk of staying silent.

WHAT PSYCHOLOGICAL SAFETY ACTUALLY MEANS

The term comes from Harvard researcher Amy Edmondson, who has spent decades studying how teams function. Her book *The Fearless Organization* details how psychological safety transforms team performance. Psychological safety, in her definition, is a shared belief that the team is safe for interpersonal risk-taking.[1,2]

Let's look at that.

"Shared belief" means it's not just individual perception. It's a characteristic of the team environment that people collectively recognize. Everyone knows whether it's safe to speak up.

"Safe for interpersonal risk-taking" refers to the specific risks involved in interacting with others: asking questions, admitting mistakes, offering ideas, raising concerns, disagreeing, and asking for help. These are all vulnerable acts. They all carry the possibility of negative consequences: looking inadequate, being blamed, facing ridicule, damaging your reputation, or hurting your career.

Psychological safety is the degree to which people believe these risks are acceptable to take. In high-safety environments, people speak up freely. In low-safety environments, they self-censor, manage impressions, and protect themselves by staying quiet.

Psychologically safe teams often have more conflict, not less, because people feel free to disagree and debate. So, the safety isn't about comfort. It's about consequences: Will I be punished, humiliated, or marginalized for speaking up? Or will I be heard, even if people ultimately disagree with me?

WHY THIS MATTERS FOR HOSPITALITY

Edmondson's research consistently shows that psychologically safe teams learn faster, innovate more, perform better, and make fewer catastrophic mistakes.[3,4] But there are reasons it matters particularly in hospitality.

The judgment we're asking for requires it. Chapter 10 described moving from scripts to frameworks, from compliance to judgment. That works only if people feel safe exercising judgment. If using your judgment and being wrong gets you punished, people will retreat to scripts. Following the script is safe. It provides cover. If the outcome is bad, at least you did what you were told to do. Judgment requires psychological safety to flourish.

Guest needs are unpredictable. Guests arrive with situations the manual didn't anticipate. Meeting those needs requires team members to improvise, make decisions without checking with supervisors, and take actions that might or might not be right. If the environment punishes mistakes, people play it safe. They defer decisions upward. They stick to what's explicitly authorized. The service becomes rigid precisely when flexibility is needed.

Problems need to surface quickly. In hospitality, small problems become big problems fast. A misunderstanding becomes a complaint becomes a social media post becomes a reputation issue. The earlier the problems surface, the easier they are to resolve. But problems only surface quickly if people feel safe raising them. In fear-based environments, problems get hidden, minimized, or passed along to the next shift.

Innovation happens at the edges. The people closest to guests see things leadership misses. They have ideas for improvements and observations about what's working and what isn't. In psychologically safe environments, this intelligence flows upward and gets acted on. In unsafe environments, it stays trapped in the heads of people who've learned that speaking up isn't worth the risk.

Emotional labor requires safety. In chapter 8, we covered how service work involves constant emotional labor. That labor is harder in environments where you're also managing fear. When you're worried about internal threats (how your manager perceives you or whether you'll be blamed for something), you have less capacity for external demands (what guests need from you). Psychological safety frees up emotional resources for actual service.

THE INTERNAL-EXTERNAL CONNECTION

Psychological safety in the team environment and internal safety (the "best friend voice" versus "bully voice" dynamic) reinforce each other.

When your internal voice is harsh and critical, you're already operating from a defensive position. External threats feel amplified. The environment doesn't have to be very unsafe for you to perceive it as dangerous because you're already under attack from inside.

When the external environment is unsafe, it strengthens the "bully voice." The criticism you fear from others validates the criticism you're already giving yourself. The environment confirms your worst beliefs about your inadequacy.

The reverse is also true. When you've developed a strong "best friend voice," you're more resilient to external threats. You have an internal foundation that doesn't collapse when someone criticizes you. When the environment is genuinely safe, it supports the internal work. External acceptance makes self-acceptance easier.

The individual work (Part Two) and the organizational work (Part Four) complement each other. Individuals working on their internal voice in toxic environments face an uphill battle. Safe environments populated by people with harsh internal critics never quite achieve the trust and openness that's possible.

The goal is alignment: internal safety and external safety reinforcing each other, creating conditions where people bring their full capability to the work.

HOW SAFETY GETS DESTROYED

Safety is destroyed faster than it's built. Understanding what destroys it helps leaders avoid the most common traps.

Punishing mistakes: This is the most obvious safety-killer. When mistakes lead to blame, humiliation, write-ups, or termination, people learn to hide mistakes rather than surface them. They also learn to avoid taking risks that might lead to mistakes, which means avoiding the judgment and initiative that excellent service requires.

Note: This doesn't mean mistakes have no consequences. It means the response to mistakes focuses on learning and improvement rather than punishment and blame. There's a difference between "What happened, and how do we prevent it next time?" and "Whose fault is this?"

Shooting the messenger: When people who raise concerns or deliver bad news are treated as problems themselves, the message is clear: *Don't bring us problems.* So, people stop. The problems don't disappear. They just go underground until they're too big to hide.

Inconsistent reactions: When leaders are unpredictable (supportive one day, punitive the next), people become hypervigilant. They can't relax because they never know which reaction they'll get. Even occasional negative reactions can destroy safety built over months of positive ones.

Public criticism: Criticizing someone in front of others, whether peers or guests, is deeply unsafe. It signals that your reputation is not protected, that your mistakes will be displayed, or that you might be next. Even people who aren't the target become less safe when they witness public criticism.

Dismissing input: When people offer ideas or raise concerns and are ignored, talked over, or dismissed ("*That's not how we do things,*" "*You don't understand the bigger picture,*" or "*Just focus on your job*"), they learn their input isn't wanted. After a few dismissals, they stop offering.

Micromanagement: Excessive oversight signals distrust. When every decision requires approval or when every action is monitored and evaluated, people understand they're not trusted to use their own judgment. They become passive, waiting for direction rather than taking initiative.

Favoritism: When some people are given safety (their mistakes are forgiven, their input is valued), while others aren't (held to higher standards, their input is ignored), the overall environment becomes unsafe. People know that safety is conditional, dependent on being in the right group or having the right relationship with leadership.

Inconsistency between words and actions: This is demonstrated by leaders who say "My door is always open" but react poorly when people walk through it, or by organizations that claim to value feedback but retaliate against those who give it. The gap between stated values and actual behavior destroys trust and safety.

BUILDING IT BACK

Building safety is slower than destroying it. It requires consistent behavior over time, not a single initiative or announcement.

Start by modeling vulnerability. Leaders who admit their own mistakes, uncertainties, and limitations make it safe for others to do the same. "I got that wrong" from a leader is powerful. It signals that being wrong is survivable, perfection isn't required, and the leader is human, too.

How you respond to bad news matters enormously. Responding with curiosity ("Tell me more about what happened") rather than blame ("How could you let this happen?") builds safety. Thanking people for raising concerns, even uncomfortable ones, reinforces that speaking up is valued.

Don't just wait for people to speak up. Actively invite input. Create structures that make input expected rather than exceptional. "What am I missing?" "What concerns do you have?"

"What would you do differently?" These questions, asked consistently and responded to well, build safety.

Then follow up. When someone raises a concern or offers an idea, circle back. Let them know what happened with it. Even if the answer is "We considered it and decided not to move forward. Here's why," the follow-up signals that input matters and is taken seriously.

Normalize learning from mistakes. Make debriefs routine, focused on learning rather than blame. Celebrate when someone catches their own mistake. Share stories of mistakes that led to improvements. Create a culture where mistakes are expected parts of growth, not shameful failures to be hidden.

Protect people from the consequences of good-faith errors. When someone makes a mistake while genuinely striving to do the right thing, protect them. This doesn't mean there is no conversation about what to do differently. It means they don't face punishment for taking reasonable risks that didn't work out.

Be consistent. Safety comes from predictability. People need to know what to expect. Leaders who are consistent in how they respond to problems, feedback, mistakes, and disagreement create environments where people understand the rules and believe them.

When someone behaves in ways that undermine safety (public criticism, shooting messengers, or creating fear), address it directly. Allowing unsafe behavior to continue signals that it's acceptable. Other people are watching.

PSYCHOLOGICAL SAFETY AND HIGH STANDARDS

A common misconception is that psychological safety means lowering standards, that being "nice" requires accepting mediocrity, or that people need to be pushed and pressured to perform, and safety undermines that pressure.

In reality, it's the opposite.

Psychological safety and high standards aren't opposites. They're partners. In fact, you need both to achieve excellence.

Without safety, high standards produce fear. People meet the minimum to avoid punishment but don't bring discretionary effort. They don't take risks that might lead to exceptional outcomes because the downside of failure is too severe. They hide struggles rather than seeking help. Performance clusters around "good enough to stay out of trouble."

Without high standards, safety produces comfort. People feel good but don't push themselves. There's no urgency for improvement. Performance clusters around "good enough to avoid effort."

With both safety and high standards, something different happens. People feel secure enough to stretch, take risks, admit when they're struggling, and ask for help. They're not protecting themselves. They're pursuing excellence. The safety frees them to focus on the work rather than on managing how they're perceived.

This combination, Edmondson calls it the "learning zone," is where the best teams operate. High expectations are clearly communicated. There is an environment where people feel supported in reaching for those expectations, even when they fall short along the way.[5]

The leader's job is to hold both: to communicate clearly what excellence looks like and to create an environment where pursuing excellence is safe.

THE MANAGER'S DILEMMA

For some frontline managers, psychological safety creates a genuine tension.

They're accountable for results. When team members make mistakes, the manager often bears the consequences. There's pressure from above to maintain standards, hit numbers, and avoid complaints. That pressure creates an incentive to control, prevent mistakes by limiting autonomy, and come down hard on errors so they don't recur.

At the same time, everything we've discussed about building capable, engaged teams requires the opposite: trusting people, accepting mistakes as learning opportunities, and fostering a culture of risk-taking.

Managers often feel caught between what senior leadership wants (results, consistency, and no problems) and what teams need (safety, autonomy, and room to grow).

This is where organizational support for managers becomes essential. Senior leaders who want psychologically safe frontline teams need to foster psychological safety among managers themselves. Managers who feel unsafe (punished for team mistakes, pressured for results without support for development, or caught between competing demands) pass that unsafety down to their teams.

The same principles apply at every level. Safety cascades. So does fear. True psychological safety happens when everyone is on the same page and speaking the same language, from ownership down to overnight housekeeping.

MEASURING PSYCHOLOGICAL SAFETY

How do you know if your environment is psychologically safe? Here are some indicators:

What happens when mistakes occur? Watch the response to errors. Is the focus on blame or learning? Do people hide mistakes or surface them quickly? Is there a difference between how leaders say mistakes are handled and how they're actually handled?

How do meetings sound? In safe environments, multiple voices participate. People ask questions, raise concerns, and disagree respectfully. In unsafe environments, the same people talk while others stay silent. Meetings are performances rather than genuine discussions.

What questions do people ask? In safe environments, people ask "dumb" questions because they know there's no penalty for not knowing something. In unsafe environments, people stay quiet rather than reveal gaps in their knowledge.

How is feedback received? In safe environments, people thank you for feedback, even critical feedback. In unsafe environments, feedback is defended against, explained away, or met with visible discomfort.

What happens to messengers? Track what happens to people who raise concerns or deliver bad news. Are they appreciated or marginalized? Do they continue raising concerns, or do they go quiet?

What do exit interviews reveal? People leaving often feel safe enough to be honest. Patterns in exit interviews can reveal safety problems that don't surface during employment.

What does anonymous feedback show? When anonymity is guaranteed, what do people say about the environment? The gap between what people say publicly and what they say anonymously indicates the level of safety.

BUILDING SAFETY IN HOSPITALITY CONTEXTS

Hospitality has some specific challenges for psychological safety.

Guest-facing pressure: When something goes wrong in front of a guest, there's urgency to assign blame and assure the guest that it won't happen again. This pressure can undermine safety if "accountability" becomes "finding someone to punish."

High turnover: Constant team changes make it harder to build the consistent relationships that support safety. Each new person has to learn whether the environment is safe, and each departure can shift the dynamic.

Physical dispersion: Teams spread across properties, shifts, and departments may not interact enough to build the trust that underlies safety. What one manager models may be different from what another does.

Power dynamics with guests: "The guest is always right" culture can position team members as always wrong by default. This undermines safety because team members know they'll be blamed in any guest-related situation.

Speed and volume: The pace of hospitality work can leave little time for the conversations that build safety: debriefs, feedback discussions, and genuine check-ins. When everything is urgent, relationship-building gets squeezed out.

These challenges are real but not insurmountable. They mean that building psychological safety in hospitality requires more intentionality, not that it's impossible.

Conduct pre-shift huddles that include "What concerns do you have about today?" Build in safety check-ins. Have post-incident debriefs that focus on learning rather than blame. Protect team members against guest behavior that crosses the line. Emphasize the need for managers to take time for one-on-ones despite the pace. Insist on consistent messaging across all managers about how mistakes are handled.

The structures matter, but what matters more is what happens in the thousands of small moments: how a manager responds when someone admits an error, how a concern gets received, or what happens after someone takes a risk that doesn't work out. Safety is built or destroyed in these moments, regardless of what the official culture says.

MARCUS'S STORY, REVISITED

Let's return to Marcus, who remained silent as he saw the child's allergic reaction develop.

In a psychologically safe environment, what would have been different?

Marcus would have felt safe to interrupt, even if he was wrong. He would have known that raising a concern, even an incorrect one, was valued rather than punished. The possibility of a guest complaint wouldn't have outweighed the chance to help, because he would have trusted his manager to have his back.

He might have said: "I apologize for interrupting, but I wanted to mention that I noticed some hives on your child's arms. I'm sure you're aware, but just wanted to make sure in case it's helpful."

The parents might have thanked him. Or they might have been annoyed or told him they had it handled. But the information would have been shared. The risk Marcus perceived (speaking up and being wrong) would have felt smaller than the risk of staying silent.

This is what's at stake with psychological safety. It's not about comfort or niceness. It's about whether valuable information flows freely, whether people bring their observations and concerns forward, and whether the organization has access to what its people know.

Marcus had information that could have helped. The environment he worked in made sharing that information feel too risky. That's a system failure, not a personal one.

Building psychologically safe environments is how we prevent the next Marcus from facing the same impossible calculus.

CHAPTER 12

THE LEADERSHIP SHIFT

Everything we've explored in this book so far comes down to this: leadership.

The internal voice work, the energy management, the four dimensions of wellness, the move beyond mechanical service, the building of psychological safety. None of it happens without leaders who understand what's needed and commit to making it real.

Adding wellness initiatives won't get you there. Neither will softer performance reviews nor more team-building activities. This requires a fundamental shift in what leaders believe their job actually is.

The traditional view: Leaders exist to ensure people do their jobs correctly. They set expectations, monitor performance, correct deviations, and manage accountability. Their primary tools are direction, oversight, and consequences.

The shift: Leaders exist to create conditions that enable people to do their best work. They build environments where worth flourishes, judgment develops, and people bring their full capability because it's safe to do so. Their primary tools are trust, development, and support.

Same title. Same organizational chart. Completely different understanding of the role.

Think of it as the difference between handing your team a map and handing them a compass. A map dictates every turn. It's efficient when the route is predictable, but the moment conditions change, a wrong turn, an unexpected detour, the map becomes useless. A compass works differently. It points north and trusts the person holding it to navigate. The destination is clear. The path to get there is theirs.

Leaders operating from the traditional model hand out maps. Every interaction is scripted, every decision pre-approved, every deviation corrected. Leaders who make the shift hand out compasses. They make the values clear, the boundaries known, and the destination understood, then give their people the room to find their own way there.

WHY THE TRADITIONAL APPROACH PERSISTS

The command-and-control model of leadership has been around for centuries. It persists because it offers something valuable: clarity and control.

Leaders know what they're supposed to do: set direction, make decisions, and ensure compliance. Team members know what they're supposed to do: follow directions, meet expectations, and stay out of trouble. The hierarchy is clear. The accountability is clear. Everyone understands their role.

This model also produces predictable results, not necessarily excellent results, but predictable ones. When you tightly control inputs, outputs stay within a narrow range. You might not get breakthrough performance, but you won't get catastrophic failure either. For risk-averse organizations, this trade-off feels acceptable.

Honestly, this model works well enough in certain contexts. When the work is truly routine, judgment isn't required, and consistency matters more than excellence, command-and-control produces adequate outcomes efficiently.

The problem is that hospitality isn't that context.

Hospitality requires judgment, creativity, genuine human connection, and the ability to respond to unpredictable situations. It requires people to bring themselves to the work, not just their compliance. Command-and-control leadership produces exactly the wrong outcomes: disengagement, mechanical service, hidden problems, and talented people heading for the door.

WHAT THE SHIFT ACTUALLY REQUIRES

Moving from traditional leadership to worth-centered leadership isn't a technique change. It's a belief change.

From "people need to be managed" to "people want to contribute."

Traditional leadership assumes that without oversight, people will slack off, cut corners, and pursue their own interests at the expense of the organization's. This assumption drives the need for monitoring, rules, and consequences.

Worth-centered leadership starts from a different assumption: Most people genuinely want to do good work. They want to contribute. They want to feel proud of what they accomplish. When they're not bringing their best, something in the environment is getting in the way.

This isn't naive optimism. Some people truly don't want to contribute, and those people need to be managed out. But treating everyone as if they're looking for ways to avoid work creates exactly the disengagement you're hoping to prevent. The assumption becomes self-fulfilling.

From "mistakes are failures" to "mistakes are information."

Traditional leadership treats mistakes as problems to be prevented and, when they occur, as failures requiring accountability. The goal is zero errors.

Worth-centered leadership treats mistakes as inevitable parts of learning and improvement. The goal is to create an environment where mistakes surface quickly, get addressed constructively, and lead to learning that prevents recurrence. Prevention of every mistake isn't the point.

From "emotions are irrelevant" to "emotions are data."

Traditional leadership often treats the emotional dimension as outside the scope of work. How people feel is their business. What matters is what they do.

Worth-centered leadership recognizes that how people feel directly affects what they do and how well they do it.

Emotional states are information about what's working and what isn't. A leader who ignores the emotional dimension is flying blind.

THE SKILLS THIS REQUIRES

The shift in belief has to translate into a shift in behavior. Here are the skills "worth-centered" leaders develop.

Deep listening: Actually hear what someone is saying, including what they're not saying, and understand their perspective, their concerns, and their experience. This is harder than it sounds, especially for leaders accustomed to moving fast and solving problems quickly.

Powerful questions: Use questions that open thinking rather than close it, and that help people discover their own answers rather than extract the answer the leader already has in mind. "What do you think we should do?" "What are you noticing?" "What would need to be true for that to work?" "What concerns you about this?"

Comfortable silence: Resist the urge to fill every pause with your own voice. Give people time to think, formulate responses, and gather courage to say something difficult. The leader who dominates the conversation crowds out everyone else.

Feedback that develops: Move beyond "good job" and "that was wrong" to feedback that helps people grow. Provide specific observations, impact of behavior, questions that prompt reflection, and genuine dialogue about improvement. Feedback as a gift rather than judgment.

Modeling vulnerability: Admit mistakes, uncertainties, and limitations. Show that being human is acceptable. This requires actual vulnerability, not performed vulnerability. People detect the difference instantly.

Holding both support and challenge: Embrace the ability to communicate "I believe in you and I'm on your side" while simultaneously holding reasonable expectations. It's neither coddling nor demanding. It's caring and expecting excellence.

Systems thinking: See beyond individual performance to the systems and conditions that produce performance. When someone is struggling, ask, "What in the environment is contributing to this?" not just "What's wrong with this person?"

Emotional regulation: Managing your own emotional responses so you don't create fear in others. This doesn't mean suppressing emotions or being inauthentic. It means not letting your frustration, anxiety, or disappointment leak onto your team in ways that undermine safety.

WHAT THIS LOOKS LIKE IN PRACTICE

Let's trace how a worth-centered leader handles some common situations differently.

A team member makes a mistake that affects a guest.

Traditional approach: Identify what went wrong. Explain the correct procedure. Document the error for accountability. Follow up to ensure the mistake isn't repeated.

Worth-centered approach: Create space to understand what happened. "Walk me through your thinking when you made that decision." Listen for what the team member was working to accomplish, what information they had, and what pressures they felt. Address the immediate guest impact, then debrief: "What would you do differently next time? What would have helped you make a better decision in the moment? Is there something about our systems or communication that contributed to this?" Focus on learning and prevention rather than blame and punishment.

The outcome: In the traditional approach, the team member learns to avoid getting caught. In the worth-centered approach, the team member learns to make better decisions and feels supported rather than shamed.

A team member brings you a problem.

Traditional approach: Take the problem. Solve it efficiently. Return the solution. Move on to the next issue.

Worth-centered approach: Resist the urge to solve immediately. "What do you think would work best? What options do you see? What do you think we should do?" Coach them toward developing their own solution. Offer your perspective as input to their thinking, rather than as the answer. If they genuinely need you to decide, decide, but default to developing their capability rather than demonstrating yours.

The difference: In the traditional approach, the leader becomes a bottleneck, and the team member stays dependent.

In the worth-centered approach, the team member builds judgment, and the leader builds capacity.

A team member seems disengaged.

Traditional approach: Have a conversation about expectations. Make it clear that performance needs to improve. Document the conversation, and follow standard HR guidelines if behavior doesn't change.

Worth-centered approach: Get curious before getting corrective. "I've noticed you seem less engaged lately. What's going on for you?" Listen without an agenda. Explore whether something in the work environment, the role, their life circumstances, or the relationship is contributing. Look for the root cause rather than just addressing symptoms. Support them in addressing whatever is getting in the way.

What changes: In the traditional approach, you might get short-term compliance, but the underlying issue remains. In the worth-centered approach, you have a chance to actually address what's happening, which might reveal a systemic issue affecting others, too.

A team member is struggling despite clear effort.

Traditional approach: Provide additional training. Clarify expectations. Check in more frequently to offer support. If improvement doesn't come, begin formal performance conversations.

Worth-centered approach: Get curious about it. Someone who applied for a front desk position might actually thrive in the back office if they're introverted and drained by constant face-to-face interactions. The extrovert buried in back-office work might come alive as a concierge. Ask: "Where do you feel most energized in this work? Where do you feel most drained?" Look for alignment between the person and the role, not just compliance with the role as assigned.

The result: In the traditional approach, you lose good people who were simply misplaced. In the worth-centered approach, you find the right fit, which increases their value to the organization and strengthens their own sense of worth.

You need to give difficult feedback.

Traditional approach: Prepare your points. Present the feedback clearly and directly. Ensure they understand the importance of the issue.

Worth-centered approach: Consider the context. What's this person already dealing with? Is their energy ball full enough to receive this feedback productively? Start with curiosity: "How do you think that interaction went?" Often, they already know. Share your observations specifically: "I noticed ..." Share impact: "Here's why that matters ..." Invite dialogue: "What's your perspective on this?" Collaborate on improvement: "What would help you handle this differently next time?"

What happens: In the traditional approach, feedback often triggers defensiveness, and the message gets lost. In the worth-centered approach, feedback becomes a conversation that actually improves behavior.

THE HARDEST PART

The hardest part of this leadership shift isn't learning new skills. It's tolerating the discomfort of less control.

Traditional leadership provides clear evidence of doing your job: You directed, you decided, you corrected, you solved. Worth-centered leadership is less visible. You asked questions. You listened. You supported. You trusted someone to figure it out.

That trust is uncomfortable, especially at the beginning. What if they make a mistake? What if you could have done it better yourself? These questions nag at leaders making the shift, and the temptation to regain control is constant.

There's also the discomfort of slower results. Developing people takes longer than directing them. The first time someone works through a problem with your coaching, it takes three times as long as if you'd just told them what to do. The payoff comes later, when they solve problems without you, develop others the way you developed them, and when the whole team operates at a higher level.

Leaders making this shift need to tolerate short-term inefficiency for long-term capability. That requires genuine belief in the approach, not just intellectual agreement. When pressure increases, leaders default to what they actually believe. If the worth-centered approach is merely a technique layered on top of traditional beliefs, it will collapse under stress.

WHEN TRADITIONAL LEADERSHIP IS STILL NEEDED

Let's be clear: There are situations where directive leadership is appropriate.

Emergencies: When safety is at risk, immediate action is required; there's no time for development conversations. Directive leadership is necessary. In a fire, you don't coach people toward discovering the exit. You point and give clear instructions.

Clear incompetence: When someone genuinely lacks the capability for their role and development isn't working, traditional performance management becomes necessary. Worth-centered leaders still make hard decisions. They just make sure those decisions are actually necessary rather than automatic.

Early stages: New team members often need more direction before they're ready for more autonomy. Worth-centered leadership meets people where they are. Someone who doesn't yet know the basics needs teaching before they need coaching.

Non-negotiables: Some things aren't open for judgment or discussion: safety protocols, legal requirements, and core ethical standards. In these areas, compliance is the expectation, and leadership ensures it.

The shift isn't from "always directive" to "never directive." It's from "directive by default" to "developmental by default and directive when genuinely needed."

THE LEADER'S OWN WORK

Everything we've explored about individuals, the internal voice, the energy dimensions, and emotional and spiritual wellness applies to leaders, too. Maybe more so.

Leaders with harsh "bully voices" tend to create environments where that harshness spreads. Their internal criticism leaks out onto their teams. Their need to protect their own ego interferes with their ability to develop others.

Leaders who are depleted, running on empty physically, mentally, emotionally, and spiritually, don't have the resources for the patient, present work of worth-centered leadership. They default to control because it's faster. They react instead of responding. They create problems that they then have to manage.

Leaders who haven't done their own work often unconsciously replicate the environments they grew up in, professionally speaking. If their formative leadership experiences were command-and-control, that's what feels normal. Breaking the pattern requires conscious effort and often support.

This is where leadership development matters, not the content-based training that teaches techniques, but the deeper development work that helps leaders examine their beliefs, understand their patterns, and build new capabilities from the inside out.

The leader who has developed a strong “best friend voice” internally is far better equipped to offer that voice to their team. Energy management has the same effect: A leader who tends to their own reserves understands what their team needs. The same is true of meaning: It’s contagious. When you’ve found purpose in the work, you can help others find it, too.

SUPPORTING LEADERS IN THE SHIFT

Organizations that want worth-centered leadership need to support leaders in developing it.

Model it from above. Senior leaders who manage their direct reports with trust, development, and support demonstrate what’s expected. Senior leaders who manage with control, blame, and pressure undermine everything they say about wanting different leadership below them.

Create safety for leaders. Leaders need psychological safety, too. They need to be able to make mistakes as they develop new capabilities, raise concerns about pressures they’re facing, and ask for help without it being seen as weakness.

Provide development resources. Provide coaching, mentorship, training, peer learning groups, and feedback mechanisms. Leaders making this shift benefit from support structures that help them develop new skills and reflect on their progress.

Align systems. If leaders are evaluated purely on short-term results, they'll manage for short-term results regardless of what the organization says it values. Performance management, compensation, and promotion decisions all need to align with the leadership approach the organization wants.

Allow time. The shift doesn't happen quickly. Leaders need time to develop new skills, build new habits, and see the results of different approaches. Expecting immediate transformation produces frustration and regression.

Address misalignment. Leaders who aren't willing or able to make the shift, despite support and time, need to be addressed. Allowing command-and-control leadership to persist in parts of the organization undermines the shift across the organization.

THE RIPPLE EFFECT

When leaders make this shift successfully:

Team members experience being trusted, developed, and supported. Their own sense of worth grows. Their "best friend voice" gets stronger because their external environment reinforces it. They bring more of themselves to the work.

As team members develop, they begin leading themselves and each other. Peer support increases. Call-outs happen less often because people actually want to show up. Problems get solved at lower levels. The leader becomes less of a bottleneck and more of a catalyst.

When team members eventually become leaders themselves, they carry the model forward. They lead others the way they were led. The culture perpetuates itself.

This ripple effect is how organizational culture actually changes, not through initiatives or announcements, but through thousands of moments where leaders interact with team members in ways that build worth.

One leader making this shift affects their direct team. Many leaders who make this shift transform the organization. Organizations that have made this shift become known for it, attracting talent, retaining talent, and delivering the kind of service that guests feel and remember.

THE REAL WORK

Leadership is a practice, not a position.

Every interaction is an opportunity to build worth or diminish it. The response to a mistake either creates safety or destroys it. Questions either develop judgment in others or signal that judgment isn't wanted. Every moment of pressure reveals what a leader actually believes.

The shift we're describing isn't a destination to reach. It's a direction to move. No leader gets it right all the time. The goal is to get it right more often, catch yourself when you slip into old patterns, and continue to develop even as you develop others.

This is hard work. It requires self-awareness, commitment, emotional regulation, genuine care for people, and tolerance for uncertainty and imperfection. It requires believing, deeply, that the people you lead are capable of more than compliance, more than following scripts, and more than doing what they're told.

This is the work that changes everything.

When leaders shift, cultures shift. When cultures shift, service shifts. When service shifts, guests experience something different: not transactions processed, but genuine human care delivered by people who are themselves genuinely cared for.

That's the vision we've been building toward. Part Five will explore what becomes possible when individuals who've done their work and leaders who've made the shift come together: the collective confidence and shared purpose that transforms groups of individuals into true teams.

PART FIVE

FROM "I'VE GOT THIS" TO "WE'VE GOT THIS"

After decades of working with individuals and teams, we've seen that the deepest transformation doesn't happen alone. It happens in community. The shift from "I've got this" to "We've got this" changes everything.

Individual work matters. A team of depleted, internally critical, spiritually empty individuals will struggle regardless of how solid the culture is. But individual work has a ceiling. At some point, what's needed isn't more personal development. It's genuine connection with others who share your purpose.

Part Five explores what becomes possible when individuals who've done their work come together as true teams. We'll examine the sequence that makes self-empowerment real, how cohesive teams actually form, what collective confidence looks like in practice, and the "We Over Me" philosophy that ties it all together.

This is where hospitality transforms from a collection of individuals doing their best into something more: a community of people who believe in each other, support each other, and create together what none could create alone.

CHAPTER 13

THE SELF-EMPOWERMENT SEQUENCE

There's a sequence that matters here, and getting it wrong undermines everything.

We've talked about how most organizations get the order backward: training, recognition, wins, then confidence. But there's a sequence that makes this work, and it starts somewhere else.

Randy has spent over forty years understanding how people actually change, and he's adamant about this point: Self-empowerment comes first. Not confidence. Not self-esteem. Self-empowerment.

The sequence goes: Self-empowerment → Self-esteem → Confidence.

Skip a step or reverse the order, and it's as if the foundation was built on sand.

WHY THE ORDER MATTERS

Let's define our terms carefully, since these words get used loosely. All three rest on the foundation we've been building throughout this book. Self-worth, the inherent value of being human that doesn't have to be earned or proved, is what the rest of the sequence stands on.

Self-empowerment is the recognition that you have agency, that you get to make choices about how you respond to what happens to you. That your internal experience, your thoughts, your interpretations, and your emotional responses are something you have influence over, not something that just happens to you. And these lead to your actions.

Self-empowerment doesn't mean controlling external circumstances. You can't. The guest is rude: You don't control that. What you control is your internal response. How you interpret the rudeness, how you respond, what story you tell yourself about it, how long you carry it, and what you do next: That's within your domain.

Self-esteem is how you feel about yourself. How do you feel about the person who looks back at you in the mirror every morning? What is your sense of your own value and worth? When self-esteem is healthy, you experience yourself as fundamentally worthy, capable, and deserving of good things. When self-esteem is low, you feel deficient, unworthy, or always falling short.

Confidence is the belief in your ability to handle specific situations and whatever life throws at you. It's task-oriented: I'm confident I can handle that difficult guest, execute that event, and solve that problem.

Here's why the sequence matters:

If you attempt to build confidence without self-esteem, every success is fragile, and it comes across as cocky rather than confident. You might feel confident after a win, but one failure shatters it. Your confidence depends entirely on recent results, so it's constantly fluctuating based on external factors you can't control.

If you attempt to build self-esteem without self-empowerment, you're dependent on external validation. Your sense of worth rises when others approve and falls when they don't. You need constant positive feedback to feel okay about yourself. That's exhausting and unsustainable.

But if you start with self-empowerment, with the recognition that you have choice and agency over your internal experience, everything else has a foundation to build on.

Self-empowerment allows you to develop self-esteem that isn't contingent on external validation because you recognize that others' opinions don't determine your worth.

That stable self-esteem allows you to develop confidence that isn't shattered by failure because your fundamental worth isn't on the line every time you work towards something.

The sequence creates resilience. Each step supports the next.

WHAT SELF-EMPOWERMENT ACTUALLY LOOKS LIKE

Self-empowerment is recognizing the space between stimulus and response.

Something happens. You respond. Between those two moments, there's a space. In that space, you have a choice. Most of the time, we react by reflex and blow past that space so fast we don't notice it exists. The stimulus happens, and we react automatically, as if our response was inevitable.

Self-empowerment is noticing that space, recognizing it, expanding it, changing it if it no longer serves you, and learning to make conscious choices in that space rather than running on autopilot.

A guest criticizes your work harshly. The stimulus is the criticism. The automatic response might be defensiveness, shame, anger, or withdrawal. But in the space between the criticism and your response, you have choices:

How will I respond? (Defensively, apologetically, curiously?)

How will I interpret this? (Are they attacking me personally, or are they frustrated about something that isn't really about me?)

What story will I tell myself? (This proves I'm incompetent, versus this is one interaction that went badly.)

What will I do with this emotionally? (Will I carry it for hours or process it and move on?)

Self-empowerment doesn't mean controlling your initial emotional reaction. You might still feel a flash of shame or anger. That's human. Self-empowerment means recognizing that the flash isn't the whole story, that what you do next is up to you.

This is profoundly liberating. Most people walk around feeling like victims of their circumstances and their emotions. Things happen to them. They feel what they feel. They react how they react. Self-empowerment reveals that there's more choice than they realized.

It's also hard work. Autopilot is easier. Recognizing choice means taking responsibility for your choices. You can no longer blame your responses entirely on what happened to you.

CONNECTING SELF-EMPOWERMENT TO YOUR INTERNAL VOICE

In that space between what happens and how you react, a voice speaks. Self-empowerment begins by recognizing which voice is speaking the loudest: the "bully" or the "best friend." Empowerment happens when you make a conscious decision to listen to the "best friend voice," not dwelling on what you did wrong, but asking what you can do differently to achieve a better outcome. The "bully" wants to knock you down. The "best friend" wants to build you up.

BUILDING SELF-EMPOWERMENT IN TEAMS

How do leaders help their teams develop self-empowerment?

Teach the concept explicitly. People need language for what they're developing. Explaining the space between stimulus and response, introducing the idea of choice in that space, and providing a framework for understanding one's own agency. This is foundational.

Model it visibly. When leaders demonstrate self-empowerment in how they handle challenges, it becomes real.

"I noticed I was starting to feel defensive in that meeting, so I paused and asked myself what was really going on." This kind of transparency shows the internal process that others can learn from.

Debrief with empowerment questions. After difficult situations, instead of asking only "What happened?" ask "What choices did you notice you had?" and "What did you choose, and why?" This frames situations as involving choice, reinforcing the self-empowerment perspective.

Avoid rescuing. When team members are struggling, the instinct is often to solve the problem for them. But every rescue is a missed opportunity for them to experience their own agency. Support them in finding their own solutions rather than providing solutions for them.

Celebrate agency. When someone demonstrates self-empowerment by handling a difficult situation with conscious choices rather than reacting automatically, recognize it. "I noticed how you stayed calm when that guest escalated. That's not easy. What helped you do that?"

Normalize the difficulty. Self-empowerment is simple but not easy. Acknowledging that it's hard work, that everyone struggles with it, and that developing it is a lifelong practice that prevents people from feeling like failures when they react automatically rather than choosing consciously.

FROM SELF-EMPOWERMENT TO SELF-ESTEEM

Once people recognize their agency, their relationship with themselves begins to shift.

When you believe you're a victim of circumstances and emotions, self-esteem is fragile. You're at the mercy of what happens to you. Good things make you feel good about yourself. Bad things make you feel bad. Your sense of worth is a roller coaster you're not driving.

When you recognize your agency, you start to respect yourself differently. You're someone who makes choices, has influence over your own experience, and isn't just tossed around by life. That recognition builds a more stable foundation.

From that foundation, self-esteem that isn't contingent on external results starts to develop. Your worth isn't proved or disproved by each interaction. You have inherent value as someone with agency, someone who's doing the work of conscious living, regardless of whether every outcome goes your way.

This is the self-esteem that doesn't collapse when a guest complains, a project fails, or a manager is critical. It's not dependent on constant success. It's grounded in something deeper.

FROM SELF-ESTEEM TO CONFIDENCE

With stable self-esteem as a foundation, confidence develops differently.

Traditional confidence is fragile and rooted more in ego, as it's based on outcomes and external factors. I'm confident because I succeeded yesterday. But what about when I fail tomorrow? The confidence evaporates.

Confidence built on self-esteem is more resilient. I'm confident because I know my worth isn't on the line from one interaction to the next. I can do things, risk failure, and handle whatever happens. Success is great. Failure is information. Neither defines me.

This kind of confidence is what allows people to exercise the judgment we discussed in chapter 10. When your worth is secure, you can take risks. You can make decisions that might be wrong. You can handle the guest situation that has no clear script. You're not protecting yourself. You're free to focus on the work.

This is also the confidence that allows genuine connection. When you're not concerned about how you're being perceived, when your internal focus isn't on managing your image, you can actually be present with the person in front of you. Your attention is available to them rather than consumed by your own insecurity.

THE SEQUENCE IN HOSPITALITY CONTEXT

Let's trace how this sequence plays out for someone in a hospitality role.

Without the sequence: A front desk agent named Dara faces a steady stream of interactions. Some go well; some don't.

Her confidence fluctuates wildly based on how the last few interactions went. After a difficult guest, she feels incompetent and dreads the next interaction. After a successful resolution, she feels capable until the next problem. Her self-worth rises and falls with guest feedback. She takes criticism personally because it feels like proof of her inadequacy. She takes praise personally, too, needing it to feel okay about herself. She has no stable ground to stand on.

With the sequence: Dara learns about self-empowerment. She begins to notice the space between a guest's behavior and her response. She starts making conscious choices about how to interpret difficult interactions. She develops her "best friend voice" as a counterweight to the internal critic. Over time, her self-esteem stabilizes. She knows her worth isn't determined by any single interaction. From that stable foundation, she develops a new kind of confidence: not "I'll handle everything perfectly" but "I'll handle whatever comes." She takes appropriate risks, exercises judgment, and stays present with guests because her attention isn't consumed by self-protection. Difficult interactions still happen, but they don't define her.

The external circumstances are identical. The internal experience is completely different.

COMMON MISTAKES

Organizations often undermine the sequence unintentionally.

Praising outcomes instead of process: When recognition focuses entirely on results ("Great sales numbers!"), it reinforces outcome-dependent self-worth. Recognizing the choices and effort that led to outcomes ("I noticed how you stayed calm and really listened to what she needed") supports the development of self-empowerment.

Rescuing too quickly: When leaders solve every problem for their team, they communicate, "You need to be rescued." This undermines self-empowerment. The message should be "You have the agency to figure this out, and I'm here to support you."

Tolerating victim narratives: When team members consistently frame themselves as victims of circumstances, self-empowerment doesn't develop. Compassion is important, and so is gently redirecting toward agency: "That sounds really frustrating. What options do you see for how to handle situations like that?"

Skipping to confidence-building: Training programs that focus on building confidence through skill development miss the foundation. Skills matter, but without self-empowerment and self-esteem, skill-based confidence is fragile.

THE FOUNDATION FOR "WE"

Here's why self-empowerment matters for what comes next.

People who haven't developed self-empowerment tend to approach teams from a dependent or defensive position. They need the team to make them feel okay. They protect themselves within the team. They're focused on their own status, image, and security.

People who have developed self-empowerment bring something different. They're not looking to the team to fill a hole in themselves. They're not protecting their ego at the team's expense. They're able to focus on the collective because they're not consumed by individual insecurity.

This is the foundation for a genuine "We Over Me" culture, not self-sacrifice or martyrdom, where people ignore their own needs for the team, but genuine collaboration, where people who are secure in themselves can offer themselves fully to something larger.

The self-empowerment sequence isn't separate from building great teams. It's the prerequisite.

Kat's Story: The Signal

My first customer service job was at a public library, and I was terrified of the desk.

Not the work itself. I could look things up, process requests, and answer questions. What scared me were the patrons who got loud. The ones who leaned in and raised their voices when they didn't like an answer. The ones who questioned my competence when I was still learning the systems. I was young, I was green, and I didn't know how to hold my ground without either crumbling or escalating.

Every shift, I'd feel it in my body before it even happened. Someone would approach with that particular energy, and my chest would tighten. I'd get smaller. I'd stumble over words

I knew perfectly well. Afterward, I'd replay the interaction for hours, convinced I'd done something wrong.

One day, I told my supervisor. Not in a formal way. Just honestly: "I don't know how to handle people who get aggressive. I freeze."

She didn't tell me to toughen up. She didn't give me a script. Instead, she asked, "What would help you feel less alone in those moments?"

We came up with a system. If I needed someone to come stand next to me, just for presence, I'd adjust the sign on the desk. If I needed a full handoff, I'd say a specific phrase out loud: "Let me get someone who can help you further." Either way, backup would appear. No judgment, no questions.

The first time I used the signal, nothing dramatic happened. A patron was getting heated about a fine, and I adjusted the sign. My coworker, Didi, walked over, stood beside me, and just ... stayed there. She didn't take over. She didn't interrupt. But suddenly, I wasn't alone, and something shifted. I found my voice. I resolved the situation myself.

Over time, I needed the signal less, not because difficult patrons disappeared, but because I'd learned I could handle them. The safety net had given me room to build self-empowerment.

Years later, I became the person who trained new staff on exactly this. Not scripts for handling complaints, but systems for supporting each other. How to ask for help without feeling like you've failed. How to stand next to a colleague without taking over. How to build the kind of team where no one has to white-knuckle it alone.

That's the self-empowerment sequence in action. It doesn't start with, "Be more confident." It starts with, "What would help you feel less alone?" The confidence comes later, built one small success at a time.

CHAPTER 14

TEAM COHESIVENESS—BUILDING SOMETHING TOGETHER

There's a difference between a group of individuals working in proximity and a team that actually functions as one.

You've felt it. You've been on both kinds of teams. On one, you clock in, do your job, clock out. Your coworkers are pleasant enough, but you're essentially parallel players, occupying the same space, wearing the same uniform, but not really connected. On the other team, something different happens. You know who's having a hard day without being told. You cover for each other without being asked. The work feels shared in a way that makes it lighter, even when it's hard.

That second experience, genuine team cohesiveness, is what makes hospitality sustainable. It doesn't happen by accident.

Remember Kat's signal system from the previous chapter? That's team cohesiveness in action: no one white-knuckling it alone and no shame in needing backup. Just a team that's built trust into how they operate.

Most of us were taught that asking for help is a weakness when, in fact, it's a strength. In this model, it means you trust your team enough to be honest about what you need.

WHAT COHESIVENESS ACTUALLY IS

Team cohesiveness is the felt sense of being part of something together. It's the experience of "we" rather than a collection of "*me*'s."

Researchers who study teams identify two types of cohesiveness:[1]

Task cohesiveness is unity around the work itself. We're aligned on what we're striving to accomplish. We understand how our individual contributions fit together. We're committed to the shared goal and willing to work toward it together.

Social cohesiveness is unity around relationships. We actually like each other. We trust each other. There's room to be ourselves, and we care about each other's well-being beyond just whether the job gets done.

Both matter. Task cohesiveness without social cohesiveness produces teams that work well together on projects but don't support each other as humans. Social cohesiveness without task cohesiveness produces teams that enjoy hanging out but don't accomplish much. The goal is a combination of both: teams united around shared purpose and genuinely connected as people.

In hospitality, both forms of cohesiveness directly affect service quality. Task cohesiveness enables smooth coordination: the kitchen and the servers working as one, the front desk and housekeeping anticipating each other's needs, the event team executing complex logistics seamlessly. Social cohesiveness enables emotional sustainability: people who genuinely support each other through the demands of the work.

WHY HOSPITALITY MAKES COHESIVENESS HARD

Before we explore how to build cohesiveness, let's acknowledge why it's particularly challenging in hospitality environments.

Shift work: Teams don't consistently work together. You might sometimes work with different people. The team that closes isn't the team that opens. Building relationships requires time together, and hospitality schedules often make that difficult.

High turnover: Just as team bonds form, people leave. New people arrive, and the dynamic shifts. Constant turnover makes it hard to build the trust and familiarity that cohesiveness requires.

Physical separation: Teams are often spread across large properties. The housekeeper on the fifth floor may never interact with the one on the third floor. The server in the restaurant doesn't cross paths with the front desk agent. Cohesiveness requires contact, and many hospitality structures limit contact.

Pace and pressure: When you're slammed, there's no time for the conversations that build relationships. You're focused on getting through the rush. The moments where connection might happen get squeezed out by operational demands.

Diverse backgrounds: Hospitality teams often include people from vastly different life circumstances, cultures, languages, and expectations. This diversity is a strength, but it also means shared understanding doesn't come automatically.

Competition for shifts, tips, and recognition: When team members compete for limited resources, cohesiveness suffers. Why invest in a relationship with someone who might get the shift you wanted?

These challenges are real. They mean that cohesiveness in hospitality requires deliberate effort. It won't emerge naturally from the structure of the work.

THE ELEMENTS OF COHESIVE TEAMS

Team cohesion comes from several elements working together.

Shared purpose: The team knows what they're collectively striving to accomplish and believes it matters. This is not just individual goals ("I want to get through my shift"), but shared goals ("We're creating an experience that matters for the people who stay here"). Purpose creates unity because everyone is pulling in the same direction.

Clear roles: Each person understands what they contribute and how it connects to others' contributions. There's no confusion about who does what. The pieces fit together without stepping on each other.

Mutual accountability: Team members hold themselves and each other accountable. It's not in a punitive way, but in a "We're in this together, and we all need to do our part" way. People follow through on commitments because they don't want to let the team down.

Trust: Team members believe that others will do what they say, will have their back, and will not undermine them. This trust has to be earned through consistent behavior, but once established, it's the foundation for everything else.

Psychological safety: We covered this in chapter 11, but it's worth emphasizing: Cohesiveness requires safety. If people don't feel safe being themselves, making mistakes, or speaking up, they hold back. They stay superficially connected but never truly integrate into the team.

Genuine relationships: People know each other as people, not just as job functions. They know something about each other's lives, care about each other's well-being, and have shared experiences and memories that create bonds.

Positive interactions: The ratio of positive to negative interactions matters enormously. Research suggests teams need multiple positive interactions for every negative one to maintain cohesion. In environments where interactions are mostly critical, corrective, or stressful, cohesiveness erodes.

Shared experiences: Teams that have been through things together, handled crises, celebrated wins, and navigated challenges develop bonds that teams without those experiences lack. Shared history creates shared identity.

BUILDING SHARED PURPOSE

Purpose is the anchor. When a team is clear on why their work matters, cohesiveness develops more naturally.

The problem is that purpose often gets lost in the daily grind. You know, abstractly, that hospitality work involves caring for people. But when you're on your thirtieth room, your fiftieth cover, or your hundredth check-in, the purpose fades. It becomes "getting through" rather than "serving."

As an ultramarathon runner once said, "I don't run one hundred miles. I run one mile one hundred times." Each one matters. The same is true in hospitality. Each guest, each room, each interaction is its own moment.

Leaders keep purpose alive through consistent reinforcement.

Tell stories of impact. Regularly share stories of guests who were genuinely helped, experiences that mattered, and moments that made a difference. These stories remind the team what their work actually accomplishes.

Connect tasks to meaning. When assigning work, connect it to purpose when possible. The approach is not just "We need to turn these rooms" but "We have a family arriving tonight for their first vacation in three years, and they're going to walk into a space we've prepared for them."

Make impact visible. Find ways to show the team the effect of their work. Guest comments, thank-you notes, return visit data, moments captured on camera. When people see their impact, purpose becomes concrete rather than abstract.

Revisit purpose in difficult moments. When the team is struggling, return to the why. "I know this is hard. Let's remember what we're actually doing here and for whom." Purpose provides perspective that helps teams push through challenges.

Involve the team in defining purpose. Purpose that's handed down from above feels different from purpose the team has articulated for themselves. Facilitating conversations about "What do we actually want to be known for?" and "What kind of experience do we want to create?" builds ownership.

BUILDING TRUST

Trust is the currency of cohesiveness. Without it, everything is a transaction. With it, genuine collaboration becomes possible.

Trust is destroyed quickly through violation. Leaders influence trust in several ways:

Be consistent yourself. Leaders who say one thing and do another destroy trust. Leaders who are predictable in their behavior, whose word means something, and who follow through on commitments, build it.

Create opportunities for small trust-building. Trust develops through experience. Small moments of reliability (covering a task, following through on a promise, sharing useful information) accumulate into genuine trust. Leaders can create these opportunities deliberately.

Address trust violations directly. When trust is broken, between team members or by leadership, addressing it directly rather than pretending it didn't happen is essential. Unaddressed violations fester and poison the environment.

Extend trust first. Trust is sometimes caught in a standoff: I'll trust you when you prove you're trustworthy, but you're waiting for me to prove the same. Leaders can break this by extending trust first, demonstrating that this is a trusting environment.

Facilitate repair. When relationships on the team are damaged, help repair them. Don't let conflicts go underground. Create space for honest conversation, accountability, and reconnection.

BUILDING GENUINE RELATIONSHIPS

This can feel uncomfortable in professional settings. There's often a belief that work relationships should stay professional, that personal lives are separate. But research consistently shows that teams with genuine personal connection perform better than those without.[2]

Create space for personal sharing. If practical, hold pre-shift huddles that include a quick personal check-in (not forced, but available). Plan team meals or gatherings that aren't work-focused. Provide opportunities to talk about life beyond the job. Avoid passing judgment if some are initially hesitant to share or do not consistently share. What may be at play is past experiences, personal preferences, or cultural norms that may have made this type of sharing unsafe or uncustomary. Make the space available. That way, it's there when team members are ready.

Celebrate personal milestones. Acknowledging moments such as birthdays, graduations, new babies, and achievements outside work says, "We see you and celebrate you as a whole person."

Pair people intentionally. When assigning shifts or tasks, prioritize relationship-building over operational efficiency. Sometimes pairing people who don't know each other well creates an opportunity for connection. But don't force it with people who are already in conflict. That rarely helps and often makes things worse.

Be patient with relationship development. Genuine connection takes time. It won't happen through a single team-building event. Consistent small opportunities for interaction matter more than occasional big ones.

THE BUDDY SYSTEM AND MENTORSHIP

One specific practice that builds cohesiveness is pairing people intentionally for mutual support.

Onboarding buddies: Pair new team members with experienced ones, not just for training but for relationship. Give them someone who checks in, answers questions, helps them figure out the social dynamics, and advocates for them. This accelerates integration into the team.

Shift buddies: These are pairs who regularly work together and develop the shorthand and anticipation that comes from familiarity. They know each other's strengths and weaknesses, naturally cover for one another, and function as a unit within the larger team.

Mentorship: More experienced team members guide less experienced ones, not just on tasks but on career development, navigating challenges, and growing in the role. This creates connection across experience levels and transfers wisdom.

Cross-training partners: People from different departments learn each other's roles, build relationships across silos, and create appreciation for what others contribute.

The common element is pairing people who wouldn't otherwise connect. Left to chance, people stick with those they already know. Doing it on purpose expands networks and builds cohesiveness across the whole team.

TEAM RITUALS

Cohesive teams often have rituals: repeated practices that create shared experience and reinforce identity. Find those that work best for your team.

Pre-shift huddle: Take a few minutes before service begins to connect, share information, and set intentions. This is not just logistics, but a moment of "We're about to do this together."

Wind-down: Build in informal time after a shift to decompress and connect. There's no agenda, just presence. This is often where relationships deepen.

Recognition moment: Set aside a regular time when team members acknowledge each other's contributions. Peer recognition builds cohesion differently than manager recognition.

Celebration: Mark achievements, milestones, and wins together. Collective celebration reinforces collective identity.

The debrief: After challenging shifts or events, come together to process what happened, what worked, and what to learn. Shared reflection builds shared understanding.

Inside jokes: These aren't necessarily created by management, but they're a sign of cohesiveness. When teams develop their own language, references, and humor, they're creating culture. Leaders can create space for this to emerge without inauthentically manufacturing it.

Rituals work because they're repeated. One gathering doesn't build cohesiveness. Regular gatherings do. The repetition creates expectation, shared memory, and a sense of connection.

NAVIGATING CONFLICT

Cohesive teams aren't conflict-free teams. In fact, the absence of visible conflict often indicates low cohesiveness: People don't care enough or feel safe enough to disagree.

Healthy teams have conflict and navigate it constructively.

Normalize disagreement. Communicate that disagreement is expected and valued. Different perspectives improve decisions. The goal isn't to agree on everything. It's to work through disagreements productively.

Distinguish task conflict from relationship conflict. Disagreements about work (how to handle a situation or what approach to take) are healthy. Personal attacks, grudges, and relationship deterioration are not. Help teams keep conflict focused on tasks rather than people.

Teach conflict skills. Many people haven't learned how to disagree constructively. Training on listening, expressing perspective without attacking, finding common ground, and agreeing to disagree can help.

Address conflict early. Small conflicts that are ignored become big conflicts. Leaders who notice tension and facilitate resolution before it escalates maintain cohesiveness.

Model constructive conflict. When leaders disagree with team members or each other, how they handle it teaches the team what's acceptable. Modeling respectful disagreement, genuine listening, and a willingness to change your mind sets the standard.

THE COHESIVENESS KILLER: FAVORITISM

Nothing destroys team cohesiveness faster than perceived favoritism.

When some team members consistently get better shifts, more recognition, easier assignments, or more forgiveness for mistakes, the team fractures. Those not favored become resentful. Even those who are favored often feel uncomfortable. The "we" disintegrates into in-groups and out-groups.

Leaders must be vigilant about this, as favoritism often occurs unconsciously. We naturally like some people more than others, find some easier to work with, and relate to some more easily. Those natural preferences can leak into decisions without our awareness.

Examine your patterns. Who gets the good shifts? Who gets recognition? Who gets coaching versus discipline? If patterns emerge, they're visible to everyone, even if you haven't noticed them.

Use fair processes. When decisions affect team members differently (e.g., scheduling, assignments, or opportunities), use transparent processes that apply equally to all team members. This doesn't mean treating everyone identically, but it means differences are based on clear, legitimate criteria.

Explain decisions. When someone gets something others don't, explain why. Unexplained differences get interpreted as favoritism. Explained differences are interpreted as fairness.

Seek feedback. Ask team members whether they feel they are being treated fairly. Create channels for honest input about perceived favoritism.

COHESIVENESS ACROSS DEPARTMENTS

In hospitality, departmental cohesiveness is important, but so is cross-departmental cohesiveness. The guest experiences the property as one thing, not as separate silos.

The handoff from front desk to housekeeping to engineering to food and beverage is best when it feels seamless. When departments don't cohere, guests fall through the cracks. Problems get passed rather than solved. The service experience fragments.

Create cross-department connections. Have opportunities for people from different departments to work together, learn about each other's work, and build relationships.

Shared goals matter. Create goals that require department collaboration rather than just department performance. Have metrics that measure the whole rather than just the parts.

Joint problem-solving builds trust across teams. When issues arise that cross departments, bring people together to solve them rather than have managers negotiate on their behalf.

Leadership modeling sets the tone. Department leaders who collaborate visibly, speak positively of other departments, and share credit and resources model the cross-department cohesiveness they want to see.

WHEN TEAMS BECOME SILOED

A caution: Cohesiveness can go too far.

When teams become so bonded that they close off to outsiders, resist change, protect each other from accountability, or develop an "us versus them" mentality toward the organization, cohesiveness has turned into something unhealthy.

Signs that a team has become siloed:

- New team members struggle to integrate and are kept at arm's length.
- The team resists feedback or direction from outside.
- There's hostility toward other departments or leadership.
- Standards slide because team members cover for each other rather than hold each other accountable.
- The team develops an identity defined by opposition (against management, against other shifts, or against the organization).

Healthy cohesiveness is open rather than closed. The team is internally connected and externally connected to other teams, leadership, and the organization's purpose. A siloed team turns into a fortress. Healthy cohesiveness is more like a network node: strongly connected internally and also connected to the larger system.

Leaders maintain this balance by:

- Keeping communication flowing between the team and the broader organization.
- Welcoming new members deliberately rather than leaving integration to chance.
- Maintaining accountability within the team's relationships.
- Connecting team purpose to organizational purpose.

COHESIVENESS AND ENERGY

Cohesive teams are more energizing than fragmented ones.

Remember the energy ball from chapter 5? Working with people you trust, have your back, and share your purpose requires less energy than working with people you don't trust, have to protect yourself from, or feel disconnected from.

Cohesiveness is a form of energy efficiency. You spend less on internal friction and have more available for the actual work.

Investing in cohesiveness isn't a nice-to-have. It's an energy strategy. Teams that cohere sustain themselves better. They experience less burnout. They weather difficult periods without fragmenting. The relationships themselves become a source of replenishment.

When Maria (from the introduction) makes it through her difficult shift and feels less alone, that's cohesiveness providing energy. When someone has a rough day, and their teammates notice and offer support, that's cohesiveness providing recovery. When the team celebrates a win together, that's cohesiveness providing restoration.

The investment in building cohesiveness pays dividends in sustainability.

THE TRANSITION TO COLLECTIVE CONFIDENCE

Cohesiveness is the foundation. What emerges from it is something even more powerful: collective confidence.

A cohesive team likes each other, trusts each other, and works well together. A collectively confident team believes in what they can achieve together. They share a conviction that "We've got this," that goes beyond individual capability.

That collective confidence, which we'll explore in the next chapter, is what enables teams to do things no collection of individuals could accomplish. It's the multiplicative effect that transforms groups into something greater than the sum of their parts.

Cohesiveness makes collective confidence possible. You cannot believe in "we" if there isn't actually a "we" to believe in.

CHAPTER 15

COLLECTIVE CONFIDENCE—WHEN "WE'VE GOT THIS" BECOMES REAL

There's a feeling that exceptional teams have.

This isn't arrogance or bravado. It's something quieter and more powerful: a shared conviction that whatever comes, we'll handle it together.

You've experienced it, probably. When you walk into a challenging shift with a team you trust, and instead of dread, there's something closer to anticipation. It's not because the work will be easy, but because you know you're not facing it alone. You know the people beside you will do their part, adapt when things go sideways, and have your back when you need it.

That feeling has a name in research: collective efficacy. We're calling it collective confidence.

It's the shared belief among team members that the team has what it takes to accomplish its goals. Not just "I've got this" (individual confidence) but "we've got this" (collective confidence).

And it changes everything.

WHAT COLLECTIVE CONFIDENCE ACTUALLY IS

Individual confidence is a belief in your own capability. *Can I handle this guest? Can I execute this event? Can I solve this problem?*

Collective confidence expands that belief to the group. *Can we deliver exceptional service tonight? Can we handle the sold-out weekend? Can we navigate this crisis together?*

The distinction matters more than it might seem.

High individual confidence with low collective confidence produces a team of capable individuals who don't function well together. Everyone believes in themselves but not in the team. They hoard information, protect their turf, and avoid depending on others because they don't trust others to come through.

Low individual confidence with high collective confidence is rare but possible: people who doubt themselves individually but believe in what the team achieves together. This can be healthy (the team provides support that boosts individual performance) or unhealthy (individuals hide behind the collective and never develop their own capabilities).

High individual confidence with high collective confidence is the goal. This is where you have people who believe in themselves and the team, bring their own capabilities, trust that others are doing the same, and take individual responsibility while also feeling collective responsibility.

Randy saw it at Aulani, the Disney resort in Hawaii. He was walking through the lobby during a slow period and noticed three front desk staff members talking and laughing. You could feel they were a solid team.

He approached, and they asked if they could help with something. "No," he said. "I just wanted to say how great it is to see you so happy and enjoying your work."

They loved that. Then he asked each of them to share a time they made magic for a guest. Without hesitation, each one had a story ready.

That's collective confidence, not individual competence, but a team that knows they're good, knows they've got each other, and has the stories to prove it.

This combination produces something multiplicative. The team's capability exceeds the sum of individual capabilities because people work together in ways that amplify rather than merely add.

THE RESEARCH BEHIND COLLECTIVE EFFICACY

The concept comes from Albert Bandura, the psychologist whose groundbreaking work on self-efficacy transformed how we understand human motivation and performance. He recognized that, like individuals, groups develop beliefs about their collective capability, and those beliefs powerfully affect what they actually accomplish.[1]

Bandura's research across many domains, sports teams, military units, surgical teams, business teams, consistently finds that collective efficacy predicts performance beyond individual capabilities.[2]

Teams with high collective efficacy:

- Set more ambitious goals
- Persist longer when facing obstacles
- Recover faster from setbacks
- Coordinate more effectively
- Experience less internal conflict
- Achieve better outcomes

The belief itself contributes to the outcome. Teams that believe they're capable approach challenges with more energy, more creativity, and more resilience than teams that doubt themselves. The belief becomes self-fulfilling.

This doesn't mean collective confidence is magical thinking. A team that believes in itself but lacks actual competence will still fail. Belief without capability is delusion. But belief with capability produces better outcomes than capability with doubt.

HOW COLLECTIVE CONFIDENCE DEVELOPS

Collective confidence isn't declared into existence. It develops through experience and interpretation.

Shared success experiences: The most powerful source of collective confidence is actually succeeding together. When a team handles a challenging situation well, delivers an excellent event, or navigates a crisis effectively, they develop evidence-based belief in their collective capability. These experiences become reference points: "Remember when we handled that? We've got this, too."

Vicarious experience: Teams learn from watching other teams succeed. Seeing a similar team accomplish something difficult expands the sense of what's possible. "If they did it, we can, too." Sharing success stories across properties or departments builds collective confidence throughout an organization.

Verbal persuasion: What people say matters. Leaders who express genuine confidence in the team and articulate belief in collective capability influence how the team sees itself. Team members who encourage and express confidence in one another build collective belief. The language environment either reinforces or undermines collective confidence.

Emotional, mental, and physiological states: How the team feels physically, mentally, and emotionally affects collective confidence. A team that's rested, resourced, and energized approaches challenges differently than one that's depleted and discouraged. This connects directly to everything we explored in Part Three about wellness: Physical, mental, emotional, and spiritual states shape collective confidence, not just individual capability.

Interpretation of experiences: The same experience can build or undermine collective confidence, depending on how it's interpreted. A challenging event that went mostly well could be framed as "We handled that" (confidence-building), "We got lucky" (confidence-neutral), or "We barely survived" (confidence-undermining). Leaders influence these interpretations.

THE LEADER'S ROLE IN BUILDING COLLECTIVE CONFIDENCE

Leaders shape collective confidence through consistent action across many moments.

Express genuine belief. Teams sense whether leaders actually believe in them or are just saying words. Genuine confidence, grounded in actual assessment of the team's capability, communicates differently than hollow cheerleading. Express what you actually believe, and if you don't yet believe in the team's capability, work on developing that capability until you do.

Appropriately frame challenges. How challenges are introduced matters. "This is going to be really hard, and I'm not sure we're ready" undermines confidence before the challenge begins. "This is a significant challenge, and I believe we have what it takes" sets a different tone. The framing influences the approach, which influences the outcome.

Debrief for confidence. After significant experiences, how you debrief affects what the team learns about themselves. Focus debriefs on what the team did well, the capability they demonstrated, and what they're now more capable of. Address what needs improvement without allowing problems to overshadow evidence of collective capability.

Protect against confidence killers. Some factors reliably undermine collective confidence: public criticism, blame for failures, lack of resources, impossible expectations, and favoritism. Leaders who protect the team from these factors preserve the confidence that's been built.

Celebrate collective achievements. When the team accomplishes something meaningful, mark it. Celebrate it. Make it part of the team's story. These moments become the evidence on which future collective confidence rests.

WHAT UNDERMINES COLLECTIVE CONFIDENCE

Collective confidence is more fragile than individual confidence because it relies on shared beliefs. One person's doubt can affect everyone.

Repeated failure: Success builds confidence; failure erodes it. Teams that repeatedly fall short, that never get to experience genuine collective success, struggle to develop belief in themselves. That's why setting appropriate challenges matters: Teams need to succeed before they encounter experiences that might fail.

Individual failure that affects everyone: When one person's mistake creates consequences for the whole team, it affects collective confidence. The team starts doubting whether everyone will do their part. This is where psychological safety matters: Create an environment where mistakes are learning opportunities rather than cause for distrust.

Resource inadequacy: Teams that lack what they need to succeed struggle to believe they'll succeed. Understaffing, inadequate tools, and insufficient training all undermine collective confidence. Leaders who fight for resources protect collective confidence.

External criticism: When the team is criticized by guests, other departments, or leadership above, collective confidence suffers. Leaders who absorb external criticism rather than passing it directly to the team and protect the team's sense of itself help maintain confidence.

THE "ENERGY VAMPIRE" EFFECT ON COLLECTIVE CONFIDENCE

Remember the energy vampires from chapter 2? They affect collective confidence, not just individual energy.

A team member who consistently expresses doubt ("This is going to be a disaster"), cynicism ("Why are we even bothering?") or hopelessness ("Nothing ever changes around here") drains the collective belief. Their energy affects the room.

This is tricky because sometimes the skeptic is seeing something real. Sometimes things genuinely are a disaster, or efforts genuinely are futile. The question is whether the expression serves the team or undermines it.

Constructive skepticism sounds like: "I'm concerned about X. This is what I'm seeing. What do others think? How might we address this?"

Destructive skepticism sounds like: "This is going to fail. I've seen it before. Why do they keep setting us up to fail?"

The first raises a concern while maintaining collective agency. The second undermines collective confidence without offering a path forward.

Leaders address this by:

- Having direct conversations with chronically negative team members about the impact of their energy.
- Creating space for legitimate concerns to be raised constructively.
- Not allowing negativity to go unchallenged in group settings.
- Building enough positive voices that negativity doesn't dominate.

Sometimes the right answer is helping a chronically negative person find a different role or a different organization. Their presence may be costing more than their contribution.

COLLECTIVE CONFIDENCE IN CRISIS

Crises are the ultimate test of collective confidence.

Teams with high collective confidence approach crises differently from teams with low confidence. They assume they'll figure it out. They trust each other to do their parts. They stay focused on the problem rather than dissolving into blame or panic. They're able to adapt because they believe adaptation is possible.

Teams with low collective confidence often make crises worse. Doubt leads to hesitation. Lack of trust leads to coordination failures. Fear leads to self-protection rather than collective effort. The crisis becomes not just the external event but also the internal dysfunction.

Building collective confidence before crises matters. You cannot build it during the crisis. The crisis reveals what's already there.

The good news is that surviving crises together builds collective confidence for future crises. Teams that successfully navigate difficulty develop a reference point: "Remember when we handled that? We've got this, too." Each survived crisis becomes evidence for the next.

Leaders support collective confidence during crises by:

- Expressing calm confidence (not false confidence, but genuine groundedness).
- Breaking the crisis into manageable pieces.
- Affirming progress as it happens.
- Reminding the team of previous challenges they've navigated.
- Modeling focused problem-solving rather than panic.

THE HANDOFF: COLLECTIVE CONFIDENCE ACROSS SHIFTS

In hospitality, work continues across shifts. The morning team hands off to the afternoon team, which hands off to the night team. How these handoffs happen affects collective confidence.

A handoff that emphasizes problems ("Good luck with 302; they've been complaining all day.") primes the receiving team for failure. A handoff that emphasizes resources ("I learned that 302 actually needs ...") primes for success.

The transition between shifts is a moment where collective confidence can be built or undermined.

Practices that build confidence across shifts:

- **Share information that enables success.** What does the incoming team need to know to succeed? Share that, clearly and thoroughly.
- **Positive framing helps when it's honest.** When things are going well, say so. When the incoming team is set up to succeed, communicate that.
- **Solidarity carries real weight.** Express confidence in the incoming team. "You've got this." "The hard part is done." "You're in good shape."
- **Avoiding dumps shows respect for the incoming team.** Don't leave messes for the next shift to clean up. Don't withhold information that would help. Treat the incoming team as teammates, not as people inheriting your problems.

When shifts feel like they're on the same team (despite never working at the same time), collective confidence extends across the whole operation. When shifts feel like separate teams (competing, blaming, and protecting themselves from each other), collective confidence fragments.

COLLECTIVE CONFIDENCE AND GUEST EXPERIENCE

Here's why this matters for hospitality: Guests feel collective confidence.

When a team believes in itself, that belief communicates. Staff seem at ease, coordinated, and like they're part of something functioning. Guests relax in that environment. They trust that their needs will be met.

When a team doubts itself, that doubt communicates, too. Staff seems stressed, fragmented, and like individuals working in proximity rather than a team working in concert. Guests sense the dysfunction. They become more demanding, more anxious, and less satisfied.

The same objective service quality plays out differently depending on the collective confidence behind it.

A team with collective confidence handles problems smoothly. There's no panic, drama, or visible scrambling. The problem gets solved with an ease that communicates competence.

A team without collective confidence handles the same problem with friction. There's uncertainty, hesitation, and visible coordination failures. Even if the problem gets solved, the process can undermine guest confidence.

Collective confidence isn't just a nice-to-have for team morale. It's a guest experience factor. The team's belief in itself becomes part of what guests experience.

BUILDING COLLECTIVE CONFIDENCE AFTER FAILURE

Failure is inevitable. No team succeeds at everything. Failure can destroy collective confidence, or it can become material for building it. The difference is in how it's processed.

Blame-focused processing destroys collective confidence. Collective belief erodes when failure leads to finger-pointing, individuals are scapegoated, or the team fractures into "Who caused this?" rather than "What do we learn?" People start protecting themselves rather than believing in the team.

Learning-focused processing can preserve and even build collective confidence. When failure leads to genuine understanding of what happened and how to do better, the team collectively owns both the failure and the path forward, and the message is "We missed this time; we'll be better next time," collective confidence survives.

Leaders facilitate learning-focused processing by:

- Resisting the urge to blame.
- Asking "What happened?" before "Who's responsible?"
- Focusing on systems and processes, not just individual behavior.
- Extracting genuine lessons and committing to applying them.
- Affirming the team's overall capability while acknowledging this particular shortfall.
- Moving forward rather than dwelling.

The best teams become more confident after failures they've processed well. They know they can face difficulties, learn from them, and improve. That resilience is itself a source of confidence.

MEASURING COLLECTIVE CONFIDENCE

There are several ways to gauge collective confidence.

Listen to the language. Teams with collective confidence use "we" language naturally. "We've got this." "We'll figure it out." "We handled harder than this." Teams without it use "I" language or, worse, "they" language that distances them from the team.

Watch the approach to challenges. Do people lean in or lean back when something difficult arises? Collective confidence shows up as willingness to engage, assumption of capability, and energy in the face of challenge.

Notice the coordination. Teams with collective confidence coordinate smoothly because they trust each other to do their parts. Teams without it have coordination friction: checking up on each other, duplicating effort, or dropping things in the cracks.

Observe crisis response. How the team responds to unexpected difficulty is revealing. Collective confidence appears as calm, focused, and coordinated action. Its absence appears as panic, blame, or fragmentation.

Check for cynicism. Cynicism is often the shadow side of low collective confidence. When people don't believe the team will succeed, they protect themselves by being dismissive. High cynicism suggests low collective confidence.

When collective confidence is established, a virtuous cycle begins.

Collective confidence leads to better performance. Better performance provides evidence that builds more collective confidence. More confidence leads to even better performance.

The team becomes increasingly capable because individuals develop and because collective belief amplifies. People bring more because they believe the team will use it well. People take risks because they trust the team to have their back. People push themselves because they don't want to let the team down.

This spiral is why some teams seem to keep getting better while others stay stuck. The stuck teams lack the collective confidence needed to improve. The improving teams have it, and each improvement reinforces it.

Starting the spiral requires deliberate effort, such as early success experiences that are carefully interpreted, leadership that expresses genuine belief, protection from confidence killers, and gradual challenge calibration that builds rather than destroys belief.

Once the spiral is running, it becomes self-sustaining. But it requires ongoing maintenance. Complacency, crisis mishandling, leader doubt, and chronic negativity can interrupt the spiral and start a downward one.

COLLECTIVE CONFIDENCE AND SELF-EMPOWERMENT

Here's how Part Five connects back to where we started.

The self-empowerment sequence from chapter 13, individual self-empowerment leading to self-esteem leading to confidence, is mirrored at the collective level.

Teams develop collective self-empowerment, the shared recognition that they have agency over their collective response to challenges. They're not victims of circumstance. They have choices. They can shape what happens.

From that collective empowerment, collective esteem develops, a shared sense that the team has worth and value, is doing what matters, and they're a team worth being part of.

From that collective esteem, collective confidence develops, the shared belief that the team is capable of meeting challenges, achieving goals, and delivering excellence.

The sequence works the same way at both levels because the underlying dynamics are the same. Agency builds worth. Worth builds esteem.

The individual and collective levels reinforce each other. Individuals with strong self-empowerment contribute to collective empowerment. Teams with collective confidence support individual confidence. The two levels spiral upward together.

CHAPTER 16

THE "WE OVER ME" PHILOSOPHY

There's a phrase Randy uses that captures something essential about what makes teams transcend mere functionality.

"We Over Me."

It's simple, but it's not easy. It's a profound reorientation that, when genuinely adopted, transforms how people experience work and how teams perform.

But it's also easy to misunderstand. "We Over Me" isn't about self-sacrifice, ignoring your own needs, or martyrdom. Those misunderstandings lead to burnout, resentment, and the opposite of what "We Over Me" actually produces.

So, let's explore what this philosophy actually means and what it makes possible.

WHAT "WE OVER ME" ACTUALLY MEANS

"We Over Me" is an orientation. It's where you habitually focus your attention and what you habitually prioritize.

The "Me" orientation asks: *What's best for me in this situation? How does this affect me? What do I need? What's in it for me?*

The "We" orientation asks: *What's best for us in this situation? How does this affect the team? What do we need?*

Someone operating from "We Over Me" processes every situation through collective impact first. They're tracking how decisions affect the team, what the team needs, and how they might contribute to collective success. Their individual success is meaningful in the context of the team's success.

This doesn't mean the "We Over Me" person ignores their own needs. It means they hold their needs within a larger frame. Their needs matter, and so do everyone else's. The collective becomes the primary unit of concern, with individuals (including themselves) as valued parts of that collective.

Think of it like ignoring a pain in your knee. Leave it untreated, and it affects how you walk, which strains your hip, which tightens your back. One unaddressed need ripples through the whole system. The same is true here: Not taking care of yourself affects the collective.

WHAT "WE OVER ME" IS NOT

Before defining what it is, let's clear away what it isn't.

It's not self-neglect. "We Over Me" doesn't mean your needs don't matter. Everything we explored in Part Three about physical, mental, emotional, and spiritual wellness remains essential. You need to take care of yourself. A depleted team member operating from marble-sized energy isn't serving the "We." They're just burning out. Think of the airplane safety message: Put on your own mask first before assisting others. The same principle applies here.

It's not losing your identity. "We Over Me" doesn't mean becoming an interchangeable unit, suppressing what makes you distinctly you. Teams need individuals who bring their unique perspectives, skills, and personalities. Randy has a team-building exercise to reinforce the concept that everyone on the team has a role and that when each person does their part, the team succeeds. The exercise is called "If we're all quarterbacks, who's going to catch the ball?" and it illustrates how a great quarterback is only great when they have a great offensive line and great receivers. The "We" is enriched by distinct "Me's," not by people who've erased themselves.

It's not conflict avoidance. "We Over Me" doesn't mean keeping quiet to maintain harmony. Sometimes serving the team means raising difficult concerns, disagreeing with the direction, or advocating for change. Healthy conflict serves the "We" better than false peace.

It's not martyrdom. "We Over Me" doesn't mean endlessly sacrificing yourself for others who aren't reciprocating. It's not about giving until you're empty while others take. Genuine "We Over Me" is reciprocal: Everyone is oriented toward the collective, not some people serving while others consume.

These misunderstandings matter because they lead people away from the philosophy rather than toward it. When "We Over Me" is understood as self-sacrifice, it becomes unsustainable.

When it's understood as compliance, it becomes oppressive. When it's understood as losing yourself, it becomes threatening.

WHY THE SHIFT MATTERS

The shift from "Me" to "We" as the primary orientation changes everything.

How you interpret events: When something goes wrong, the "Me" orientation asks, "How does this affect me?" and often leads to self-protection, blame-deflection, or withdrawal. The "We" orientation asks, "How do we address this?" and leads to collective problem-solving.

How you approach success: When something goes well, the "Me" orientation wants credit, recognition, and personal reward. The "We" orientation seeks success that benefits the collective and is less concerned with who gets credit.

How you handle conflict: The "Me" orientation approaches conflict as a contest to win. The "We" orientation approaches conflict as a problem to solve, where the goal is the best outcome for the collective rather than victory for your position.

How you use resources: The "Me" orientation hoards resources (information, opportunities, or recognition) because having more means doing better individually. The "We" orientation shares resources because collective capability matters more than individual advantage.

How sustainable the work becomes: The "Me" orientation burns out faster because you're carrying everything yourself. The "We" orientation is more sustainable because the load is shared, the support is mutual, and the meaning is larger.

WHEN SELF-INTEREST WORKS AGAINST YOU

It sounds counterintuitive, but operating from "We Over Me" often serves your individual interests better than operating from "Me Over We."

When you orient toward the collective:

- You build relationships and trust that serve you when you need help.
- You're part of a team that achieves more than you could alone, and you share in those achievements.
- You develop a reputation as someone people want to work with, which creates opportunity.
- You experience more meaning because you're connected to something larger.
- You're more sustainable because you're not carrying everything alone.

When you orient toward yourself first:

- You may get short-term wins, but you erode relationships and trust in the process.
- You limit yourself to what you alone can accomplish.

- You develop a reputation as someone who's in it for themselves, which limits opportunity.
- You experience less meaning because you're disconnected from a larger purpose.
- You burn out faster because everything depends on you.

Here's how it works: The path that seems to serve your interests (putting yourself first) often undermines you. The path that seems to require sacrifice (putting the collective first) often serves your interests better in the long run.

This isn't an argument for fake selflessness or pretending to care about the collective while secretly being in it for yourself. That doesn't work. People sense the difference between genuine "We Over Me" orientation and its performance.

It's an observation that genuine orientation toward the collective tends to produce better outcomes for individuals than an orientation toward self. That's how it actually works.

"WE OVER ME" REQUIRES "ME" FIRST

The sequence from chapter 13 matters: self-empowerment, then self-esteem, then confidence, then "We Over Me." Each step builds the foundation for the next.

When people haven't done the inner work, they approach teams from a place of need. They're looking for validation, protection, and identity. They lean on the team rather than supporting it. What looks like team focus is actually self-focus: *What will the team give me?*

But when people have developed self-empowerment, stable self-esteem, and genuine confidence, something shifts. Each person brings something to the team and doesn't just take. They're secure enough to put "We" first without their "Me" being threatened. Collaboration becomes energizing rather than draining. Celebrating a colleague's win doesn't feel like a personal loss.

The individual work isn't separate from team building. It's what makes real teamwork possible.

THE TEAM'S ROLE IN SUPPORTING "WE OVER ME"

Individual development is necessary but not sufficient. The team environment must support a "We Over Me" orientation, or it will erode. This means reciprocity (enough people practicing it that it's mutual), protection from exploitation (addressing those who consistently take more than they give), and the psychological safety, shared purpose, and fair distribution we've already discussed. Without these conditions, "We Over Me" becomes hard to sustain. With them, it becomes the natural way of working.

"WE OVER ME" IN DAILY PRACTICE

What does "We Over Me" look like in the daily reality of hospitality work?

Helping before being asked: You notice when a colleague is overwhelmed and offer support without waiting for a request. You see what needs doing and pitch in, even if it's not "your job."

Sharing information: You pass along what you've learned about a guest, a situation, or a better way of doing something. You don't hoard knowledge that would help others.

Giving credit: When something goes well, acknowledging others' contributions rather than claiming success as purely your own.

Absorbing blame appropriately: When the team makes a mistake, you don't immediately point fingers at others. You're willing to take responsibility for collective shortfalls.

Celebrating others' wins: You genuinely rejoice when teammates succeed, without jealousy or competition. Their success is the team's success, which is your success.

Supporting new team members: You invest in helping newcomers succeed, even though it takes time and energy, because their success strengthens the team.

Maintaining positivity: You bring energy that lifts the room rather than drains it. You don't spread negativity that brings down the collective.

Putting guests first together: When a guest's need arises, you don't calculate whether it's "your" responsibility. You just handle it because serving guests is what the team does.

These practices are small individually. Accumulated across a team, they create a fundamentally different environment than "Me Over We" practices produce.

THE SHIFT FROM COMPETITION TO COLLABORATION

"Me Over We" breeds internal competition: information hoarding, reluctance to help, and blame dynamics. "We Over Me" replaces it with collaboration: information sharing, collective ownership, and celebrating each other's wins.

Both dynamics are self-reinforcing. Competition breeds more competition. Collaboration breeds more collaboration. Leaders set the cycle through how they structure incentives, recognize achievement, and model and tolerate certain behaviors.

"WE OVER ME" ACROSS THE ORGANIZATION

The philosophy extends beyond immediate teams.

Within a property, different departments are part of a larger "We." Housekeeping, front desk, food and beverage, engineering, and management are all part of the collective. "We Over Me" means departments collaborating rather than competing, sharing resources rather than hoarding, and supporting each other rather than blaming.

Across properties, the organization is the "We." Properties share best practices, support each other through challenges, and celebrate collective success rather than compete for rankings.

The philosophy scales. At every level, the question is the same: Are people oriented toward the collective or toward their unit within it?

The most functional organizations have a "We Over Me" orientation at every level: individuals oriented toward their teams, teams toward their departments, departments toward their properties, and properties toward the organization.

Most organizations are mixed: Some levels function collectively, while others fragment into internal competition. The work is extending "We Over Me" orientation wherever it's missing. This change can be difficult at first, but over time, it can be the prevailing philosophy. Be patient as it gains traction.

HOW LEADERS REINFORCE "WE OVER ME"

Leaders shape which mindset takes hold through everyday decisions. Where do your rewards go: to individuals who outperform their peers, or to teams that achieve collective goals? Are you spotlighting individual stars or celebrating what the whole team built together?

Resource allocation sends a message, too. Scarcity forces departments to compete; abundance enables sharing. The behavior you model matters as much as the policies you set, and the behavior you tolerate becomes the behavior you endorse.

At every level, leaders are either building a "We Over Me" culture or allowing "Me Over We" to take root. The question isn't whether you're influencing this dynamic. You are. The question is which direction.

WHEN "WE OVER ME" IS TESTED

The orientation is easy to maintain when things are going well. It's tested when things get hard.

During scarcity: When there aren't enough shifts, enough resources, or enough recognition to go around, the temptation to grab for yourself intensifies. A genuine "We Over Me" orientation means figuring out together how to navigate the shortage rather than each person scrambling for themselves.

During a crisis: When a crisis happens, pressure is high, and the stakes are elevated. Self-protection instincts activate, but enacting the "We Over Me" philosophy can make a huge difference to your team. Randy saw this at a luxury resort on Maui after the 2023 fires. Many team members lost their homes. Leadership didn't hesitate: They gave shelter to those staff members and their families and let them stay on the property until they could secure other housing. That is what taking care of your team looks like. Every visit before and since, Randy has noticed the same thing: Every staff member, from the front desk to housekeeping to pool services, operates from the same page. Their eyes say, "*How can I help?*" That's not just training. That's culture.

During failure: When things go wrong, the temptation is to deflect blame. A collective orientation means owning it together and learning together, rather than finding someone to sacrifice.

The same principle holds during conflict and success. Working toward what's best for the collective during disagreements, celebrating together when things go well rather than competing for recognition, are the moments that prove whether "We Over Me" is real or just aspirational.

THE SPIRITUAL DIMENSION OF "WE OVER ME"

Remember the spiritual dimension from chapter 9: connection to something larger than yourself and your immediate concerns?

"We Over Me" is partly a spiritual orientation. It involves seeing yourself as part of something larger, finding meaning in contribution to the collective, and experiencing your work as connected to shared purpose.

"We Over Me" often feels more meaningful than "Me Over We." The individual orientation is lonely. You're in it alone, accumulating for yourself, and succeeding or failing on your own. Even when you succeed, the success is hollow because it's not connected to anything larger.

The collective orientation is connected. You're part of something, your contribution matters to others, and the success and the struggles get shared. The meaning is built into the orientation itself.

This is also why people with a strong "We Over Me" orientation tend to be more resilient. When you're connected to something larger, setbacks don't hit as hard. There's perspective, there's support, and there's purpose that transcends any individual outcome.

The spiritual dimension of work, the question of meaning and purpose, is often answered through "We Over Me," not entirely (individual meaning matters, too), but substantially. For many people, being part of a genuine "We" is the answer to "*Why does this matter?*"

BUILDING "WE OVER ME" CULTURE

Name it explicitly. Give the philosophy language. Talk about "We Over Me" directly. Make it part of how the team describes itself and its values.

Model it visibly. Leaders who operate from "We Over Me" demonstrate what it looks like. Leaders who talk collectively but act individually undermine everything they say.

Hire for it. In interviews and selection, look for orientation toward collective success. Ask about team experiences. Listen for "we" language versus "I" language. People's natural orientation is visible if you're looking for it.

Orient new members. When people join, clearly communicate the "We Over Me" expectation. Help them understand that this is how the team operates. Don't assume they'll absorb it through osmosis.

Recognize it. When people demonstrate "We Over Me" behavior, acknowledge it. Celebrate examples of collective orientation. Make visible what you want to see more of.

Acknowledge collective experiences. Teams that go through significant experiences together develop stronger collective orientation. Shared challenge, shared celebration, and shared difficulty all build the "We."

One last thing worth saying: "We Over Me" is an invitation, not a demand. You don't get collective orientation by forcing it. You get it by creating conditions where it makes sense, is rewarded, is reciprocated, and connects to meaning. For people who've done their individual work, this invitation is exactly what they've been looking for. For people who haven't, it shows them why the individual work matters.

CHAPTER 17

THE FIVE PRACTICES OF COLLECTIVE CONFIDENCE

Now it's time to bring it together into something practical.

What do teams actually do, day after day, to build and maintain collective confidence? What practices, embedded in the rhythm of work, turn philosophy into lived experience?

We've identified five practices that, when consistently applied, transform groups of individuals into teams that genuinely believe in themselves and each other. These aren't occasional initiatives or annual training events. They're ongoing disciplines woven into how work happens.

Together, they represent what it looks like when worth is truly at work.

PRACTICE ONE: THE WORTH CHECK-IN

Every shift, every day, before the work begins, have a moment of honest acknowledgment.

The worth check-in is simple. In the morning meeting, ask everyone to take a moment and notice their energy level. Then, by a show of hands, whose energy ball is lit up today? Who could use some support?

This takes sixty seconds and gives you real information. When someone doesn't raise their hand for either question, that's a cue. A brief check-in after the meeting opens the door:

"I'm at about seventy percent today. Slept well, feeling pretty energetic."

"Honestly, I'm running low. Rough morning at home."

"I'm good. Ready to go. Feeling solid."

These conversations don't have to be long. The point is that people feel seen, and the team has what it needs to support each other through the shift.

When checking in becomes routine, it becomes safe to be human. The pretense that everyone is always fine dissolves. People develop the muscle of noticing their own internal state. Starting the shift with genuine sharing creates connection before the work begins. You're not just parallel players. You're people who know something real about each other today.

The worth check-in requires psychological safety to function. If sharing vulnerability leads to judgment or exploitation, people stop sharing honestly. Leaders model by going first and by responding to honesty with appreciation rather than concern.

PRACTICE TWO: THE ENERGY PROTECTION PROTOCOL

Teams that sustain collective confidence actively protect each other's energy.

This means developing shared awareness of what drains energy and creating systems to minimize unnecessary drain. It also means watching for signs of depletion in each other and intervening before the energy levels drop to marble size.

Identify common drains. What situations, interactions, or patterns reliably drain energy in your environment? Is it certain guest types? Specific operational problems? Times of day? Having shared language for these drains helps the team navigate them more consciously.

Create buffers. When possible, build recovery time after draining experiences. Don't schedule the most demanding tasks back-to-back. Create breathing room in the flow of work.

Watch for warning signs. Train the team to notice each other's depletion signals: withdrawal, irritability, or that flatness in the eyes. When you notice, check in. "You seem like you're running low. What do you need?"

Protect the break. Breaks aren't optional. They're energy recovery time. Teams that protect each other's breaks and cover so colleagues can actually step away maintain collective capacity.

The energy protection protocol recognizes that individual energy management isn't enough. The team has to function as an energy network, where protecting each other's capacity is everyone's responsibility.

PRACTICE THREE: THE VOICE-SHIFT MOMENT

When the "bully voice" gets loud, individually or collectively, teams need practices for shifting to the "best friend voice."

The voice-shift moment is a deliberate pause to notice which voice is running and to consciously choose a different narrator.

Individual application: When you notice your internal critic running hard, pause. Name it: "That's my 'bully voice.'" Then ask: "What does my 'best friend voice' say about this?" Deliberately generate the alternative narrative.

Collective application: Teams develop collective "bully voices," too: shared cynicism, collective catastrophizing, or group negativity. When someone notices the team sliding into this territory, they call it out. "Hey, we're in a collective 'bully voice' right now. What's the 'best friend' version of this situation?"

The practice requires:

Permission to name it: Team members need to feel safe saying "I think we're catastrophizing" or "That sounds like our collective 'bully voice.'" This form of speaking up requires psychological safety.

Genuine alternatives: This isn't toxic positivity or pretending everything is fine. The "best friend voice" tells the truth; it just tells it with kindness.

Practice: Like any skill, shifting voices gets easier with repetition. Teams that regularly practice, in low-stakes moments, build the muscle for high-stakes moments.

Leader modeling: When leaders visibly catch their own "bully voice" and shift to "best friend voice," they demonstrate that this is how we operate here.

The voice-shift moment is when the internal work from chapter 4 becomes collective practice. The team holds each other accountable for the quality of internal dialogue, individually and as a unit.

PRACTICE FOUR: THE COLLECTIVE WIN CAPTURE

Collective confidence builds through accumulated evidence of collective capability. But that evidence can slip by unnoticed if teams don't deliberately capture it.

The collective win capture is the practice of regularly identifying, naming, and celebrating what the team has accomplished together.

Daily capture: At the end of each shift, take a moment to name what went well. *What did we handle effectively? What guest experience did we create? What problem did we solve together?* This isn't false praise. It's honest acknowledgment of a genuine collective accomplishment.

Story banking: Collect stories of the team at its best, such as moments of exceptional service, challenges navigated, and crises handled. These stories become part of team identity, evidence for collective confidence, and onboarding material for new members.

Marking milestones: When significant collective achievements happen, mark them. Celebrate. Create a shared memory. The sold-out weekend that ran smoothly, the difficult event that came together, and the challenging period that the team got through are milestones that become reference points for future confidence.

Honest accounting: The practice is about ensuring the wins are counted alongside the losses. Many teams are better at cataloging what went wrong than what went right. The collective win capture restores balance.

The goal is building a narrative of collective capability. Teams tell stories about themselves, and those stories shape identity and confidence. The collective win-capture ensures the story includes what the team is capable of, not just what's gone wrong.

PRACTICE FIVE: THE FORWARD COMMITMENT

Collective confidence isn't just about the past. It's about the future. Teams with genuine collective confidence make commitments about what they'll do together going forward.

The forward commitment is the practice of regularly articulating what the team is committed to creating, handling, or becoming.

Before a challenge: When facing something difficult, the team decides together how they'll handle it. Articulating that shared plan out loud builds collective confidence for what's ahead.

For ongoing growth: *What is the team working on developing? What are we striving to get better at together?*

Having shared goals creates collective purpose beyond just getting through the day.

For accountability: None of this means anything without follow-through. Teams debrief against what they said they'd do: "We said we were going to create X. Did we?" This closes the loop and builds integrity.

As identity: Over time, these declarations shape who the team understands itself to be. "We're the team that handles difficult situations with grace." "We're the team that makes every guest feel individually cared for." Those statements become self-fulfilling.

The forward commitment keeps the team oriented toward what they're creating together rather than just reacting to what happens. It's the proactive expression of collective confidence, not just "we've got this," but "this is what we're going to do to make it happen."

INTEGRATING THE FIVE PRACTICES

The five practices aren't isolated activities. They work together as a system.

The **worth check-in** creates the foundation of honesty and connection.

The **energy protection protocol** ensures people have the capacity to bring their best.

The **voice-shift moment** keeps internal and collective dialogue constructive.

The **collective win capture** builds evidence-based confidence.

The **forward commitment** channels confidence toward shared purpose.

Together, they create a rhythm of collective development. Each practice reinforces the others. Teams that check in honestly are better at protecting each other's energy. Teams that protect energy are better equipped to shift voices. Teams that shift voices are more likely to notice wins. Teams that capture wins have more fuel for forward commitments. Teams that make commitments together deepen the honesty of their check-ins.

The practices also connect back to everything else in this book. The individual work (internal voice, energy management, and four dimensions) enables the practices. The organizational conditions (psychological safety, leadership approach, and moving beyond mechanical service) create space for the practices. The practices are where individual development and organizational culture meet in lived team experiences.

STARTING THE PRACTICES

How do teams begin implementing these practices?

Start with one. Don't attempt to implement all five simultaneously. Choose the practice that addresses the team's most pressing need. Build that one until it's habit, then add another.

Leaders go first. These practices typically start with leaders who introduce them, model them, and hold space for them.

Over time, ownership spreads to the team, but initial leadership is usually necessary.

Explain the why. Don't just impose new activities or procedures. Explain what they're for, how they connect to collective confidence, and why they matter. Understanding the purpose improves buy-in.

Start simple. The practices can be very brief: a two-minute check-in, a thirty-second voice-shift, or a one-minute win capture. Keep it simple enough to sustain before you make it more elaborate.

Be consistent. Repetition is what makes it work. Occasional practice is a nice idea. Consistent practice is culture change. Consistency matters more than perfection.

Adapt to context. These practices need to fit your specific environment, team culture, and operational reality. Don't implement someone else's version. Develop your own expression of each practice that works for your people.

Celebrate the practice, not just outcomes. When the team consistently engages in the practices, recognize that. The practices themselves are wins, regardless of what results they immediately produce.

WHAT THIS PRODUCES

Teams that consistently engage in these five practices develop something distinctive.

They have higher collective confidence because they're building the evidence and the commitment that underpin it.

They have more psychological safety because the practices create regular opportunities for honesty and vulnerability.

They have stronger cohesion because the practices deepen relationships and shared experience.

They have more sustainable energy because they're actively protecting each other's capacity.

They have a genuine "We Over Me" orientation because the practices embed collective focus into the rhythm of work.

They deliver better service because all of this enables the authentic presence and genuine care that clients and guests feel and remember.

This is what it looks like when worth is genuinely at work, not as a slogan or an initiative, but as lived practice. It is not something that happens once at a training, but is something that happens every shift, every day, in the small moments where teams either build or erode collective capability.

The five practices are how the philosophy becomes real.

THE WORTH@WORK JOURNEY

What we've explored throughout this book represents a journey.

It starts with individuals understanding their internal world: the voice in their head, the energy they carry, and the dimensions of wellness that need tending.

It moves to organizational conditions: the shift beyond mechanical service, the building of psychological safety, and the leadership approach that creates space for people to flourish.

It culminates in collective capability: the self-empowerment sequence, team cohesiveness, collective confidence, and the "We Over Me" philosophy that ties it all together.

This path is what we've come to call WORTH@WORK.

It's the recognition that worth, genuine inherent worth, is the foundation that makes everything else possible. When people know their worth, they show up differently. When leaders honor that worth, cultures transform. When teams operate from collective worth, service becomes something guests feel in ways they struggle to articulate but never forget.

The five practices are how teams live this out daily. But the journey itself is larger than any set of practices. It's a fundamental reorientation from performance-based value to inherent worth, from individual striving to collective flourishing, and from mechanical service to true human connection.

That reorientation is available to any team, in any hospitality environment, that commits to the work.

AFTERWORD: WHERE DO WE GO FROM HERE?

It's 11:45 p.m. on a Friday night, and Maria is still at the concierge desk.

You met her in the Introduction. She's been at this property for four years, training for the role she's always wanted, holding together a life that keeps threatening to come apart. Her husband just lost his job. Her daughter's science project sits unfinished on the kitchen table. And a celebrity guest has just arrived, unraveling over lost luggage.

We told you that story to illustrate something: that the quality of service in that moment depended entirely on what was happening inside Maria. Her internal voice. Her energy reserves. Her capacity to see beyond the surface complaint to the human being in front of her.

What we didn't tell you is what made that moment possible.

Maria didn't arrive at that interaction by accident. She'd been part of a team that had done the work. They'd learned about the "bully voice" and the "best friend voice." They'd developed practices for protecting each other's energy. They'd built the kind of psychological safety where people could be honest about struggling. They'd cultivated collective confidence through hundreds of small moments of support and shared success.

When Maria needed to reach past her own exhaustion to genuinely connect with a stressed stranger at nearly midnight, she had something to draw on, not just her own reserves, but the accumulated investment of a team and an organization that had made her capacity their concern.

That's what this book has been about.

THE CORE OF WHAT WE'VE EXPLORED

The hospitality industry is facing a crisis that traditional approaches aren't solving: turnover rates that make sustainable excellence nearly impossible, burnout that claims the best people first, and service that guests experience as technically adequate but emotionally hollow.

The root cause isn't what most organizations think. It's not inadequate training or poor hiring or insufficient accountability. It's that we've been building from the outside in when we need to build from the inside out.

Worth comes first. When people recognize their inherent value and are not constantly defending their sense of adequacy, they have attention and energy available for genuine service. The internal foundation determines the external expression.

The internal voice matters. The "bully voice" that criticizes and catastrophizes drains energy and undermines presence.

The "best friend voice," which offers perspective and kindness, creates the internal conditions for authentic connection. Learning to work with these voices is practical, trainable, and transformative.

Energy is a renewable resource, but it requires management. The energy ball expands and contracts based on how well we tend to our physical, mental, emotional, and spiritual dimensions. Individuals need to manage their own energy, and organizations need to create conditions that support rather than undermine that management.

Organizational conditions determine individual capacity. Psychological safety, a leadership approach, and moving beyond mechanical service create an environment where individual development translates into collective capability. Without supportive conditions, individual work hits a ceiling.

The shift from "I" to "We" changes everything. Self-empowerment enables self-esteem enables confidence. Cohesive teams develop collective confidence. "We Over Me" orientation transforms groups of individuals into something greater than the sum of their parts. The five practices make this lived reality rather than abstract philosophy.

This is the WORTH@WORK framework. It's not a customer service program nor is it another set of scripts and standards. It's a fundamental reorientation that addresses the actual root causes of the industry's challenges. And it works.

The math changes. When you're not constantly replacing people (at $7,500 or more per replacement) or not losing your best performers to burnout and guests return because of how your service made them feel, the financial equation shifts. Investment in worth pays returns in retention, morale, reputation, and results.

This isn't theory. We've seen it happen. The frameworks and practices in this book come from decades of real work and observation with real organizations and real people. They're grounded in research, refined through application, and validated by outcomes.

Now it's yours to use.

A FINAL WORD

We hope this book has given you frameworks for understanding what's really driving turnover, burnout, and disconnection, and for building something better. We hope it's sparked recognition, challenged assumptions, and opened possibilities. If it also feels like a lot, we understand. You don't have to overhaul everything to begin. Pick one idea, one practice, one small shift, and start there. The teams that change are not the ones that do everything at once. They're the ones that begin. Every small step toward worth moves you somewhere better than where you are today.

Most of all, we hope it's reminded you that your worth isn't earned through performance or proved through outcomes. It's already there. It's been there all along.

You matter. Your team matters. The work matters.

Now go be the reason someone's day gets better.

NOTES

Introduction

1. Adam Perkowsky, “Report: Hospitality hits all-time workforce high; turnover at crisis level,” *Hotel Business*, December 4, 2025, https://hotelbusiness.com/report-hospitality-hits-all-time-workforce-high-turnover-at-crisis-level/
2. U.S. Department of Labor Bureau of Labor Statistics, “Job Openings and Labor Turnover—February 2026” (news release, March 31, 2026), https://www.bls.gov/news.release/pdf/jolts.pdf

Chapter 1

1. Arlie Russell Hochschild, *The Managed Heart: Commercialization of Human Feeling* (Oakland, CA: University of California Press, 1983).

Chapter 2

1. Randy Haveson, *Becoming Your Own BFF: Building Self-Esteem for a Life of Joy* (2023).

Chapter 3

1. Amy F. T. Arnsten, "Stress Signalling Pathways That Impair Prefrontal Cortex Structure and Function," *Nature Reviews Neuroscience*, 10, no. 6 (2009): 410–422. https://doi.org/10.1038/nrn2648
2. Amy C. Edmondson, *The Fearless Organization: Creating Psychological Safety in the Workplace for Learning, Innovation, and Growth* (Hoboken, NJ: John Wiley & Sons, 2018).

Chapter 4

1. Randy Haveson, *Becoming Your Own BFF: Building Self-Esteem for a Life of Joy* (2023).
2. Kristin Neff, *Self-Compassion: The Proven Power of Being Kind to Yourself* (New York: William Morrow, 2011).
3. Kristin Neff and Christopher Germer, "A Pilot Study and Randomized Controlled Trial of the Mindful Self-Compassion Program," *Journal of Clinical Psychology* 69, no. 1 (2013): 28–44. https://doi.org/10.1002/jclp.21923

Chapter 6

1. A. M. Williamson and Anne-Marie Feyer, "Moderate Sleep Deprivation Produces Impairments in Cognitive and Motor Performance Equivalent to Legally Prescribed Levels of Alcohol Intoxication," *Occupational and Environmental Medicine* 57, no. 10 (2000), https://doi.org/10.1136/oem.57.10.649

2. Bruce S. McEwen, "Central Effects of Stress Hormones in Health and Disease," *European Journal of Pharmacology* 583 (2008): 174–185. https://doi.org/10.1016/j.ejphar.2007.11.071

Chapter 7

1. George A. Miller, "The Magical Number Seven, Plus or Minus Two: Some Limits on our Capacity for Processing Information," *Psychological Review* 63 (1956): 81–97. https://doi.org/10.1037/h0043158
2. American Psychological Association, "Multitasking: Switching Costs" (2006).
3. Joshua S. Rubinstein, David E. Meyer, and Jeffrey E. Evans, "Executive Control of Cognitive Processes in Task Switching," *Journal of Experimental Psychology: Human Perception and Performance* 27, no. 4 (2001): 763–797. https://psycnet.apa.org/doiLanding?doi=10.1037%2F0096-1523.27.4.763
4. Alejandro Lleras and Atsunori Ariga, "Brief and Rare Mental 'Breaks' Keep You Focused: Deactivation and Reactivation of Task Goals Preempt Vigilance Decrements," *Cognition* 118, no. 3 (2011): 439–443. https://doi.org/10.1016/j.cognition.2010.12.007

Chapter 8

1. Arlie Russell Hochschild, *The Managed Heart: Commercialization of Human Feeling* (Oakland, CA: University of California Press, 1983).

Chapter 9

1. Amy Wrzesniewski et al., "Jobs, Careers, and Callings: People's Relations to Their Work," *Journal of Research in Personality* 31 (1997): 21–33. https://doi.org/10.1006/jrpe.1997.2162

Chapter 11

1. Amy C. Edmondson, *The Fearless Organization: Creating Psychological Safety in the Workplace for Learning, Innovation, and Growth* (Hoboken, NJ: Wiley & Sons, 2018).
2. Amy C. Edmondson, "Psychological Safety and Learning Behavior in Work Teams," *Administrative Science Quarterly* 44, no. 2 (1999): 350–383. https://doi.org/10.2307/2666999
3. Amy C. Edmondson, *The Fearless Organization.*
4. Amy C. Edmondson, "Psychological Safety."
5. Amy C. Edmondson, "Psychological Safety."

Chapter 14

1. Andrey V. Sidorenkov and Evgueni F. Borokhovski, "The Role of Cohesion and Productivity Norms in Performance and Social Effectiveness of Work Groups and Informal Subgroups," *Behavioral Sciences* 14, no. 5 (2023). https://doi.org/10.3390/bs13050361
2. Ron Friedman, "High-Performing Teams Don't Leave Relationships to Chance," *Harvard Business Review*, September 14, 2022, https://hbr.org/2022/09/high-performing-teams-dont-leave-relationships-to-chance

Chapter 15

1. Albert Bandura, *Self-Efficacy: The Exercise of Control* (New York: Worth Publishers, 1997). See also: Albert Bandura, "Exercise of Human Agency Through Collective Efficacy," *Current Directions in Psychological Science* 9, no. 3 (2000): 75–78. https://doi.org/10.1111/1467-8721.00064
2. Albert Bandura, *Self-Efficacy*.

MEET YOUR CO-AUTHORS

WORTH@WORK brings together two perspectives on the same truth: When people operate from authentic worth rather than fear or ego, they create extraordinary experiences that no script could ever produce.

Randy Haveson, MA, developed the foundational concepts you'll encounter in this book: the ego vs. self-esteem continuum, the "bully voice" vs. "best friend voice," the energy ball, and the four dimensions of self. These frameworks emerged through his own journey of transformation and decades of helping others build self-esteem. He introduced them in his book *Becoming Your Own* BFF, and they have changed countless lives.

Randy writes: "*When I worked as a greeter at Walt Disney World's flagship resort, and saw a guest approaching the resort, I never once had the thought, 'Here comes another one.' Every guest was a person, not a transaction. And that wasn't something I had to force. It came from somewhere deeper.*

I've spent decades figuring out where that 'somewhere' actually is. What I've learned is that connection comes from being fully present, operating from a sense of worth rather than fear, and paying attention to the person in front of you. No script *produces that.*

If you're on the front lines, I want you to walk into work and actually want to be there. I want you to handle the difficult guest without your stomach dropping. I want you to go home at the end of a shift and still have something left for the people you love.

If you're leading a team, I want you to build the kind of environment where that's possible. I want you to stop losing your best people to burnout. I want you to create something your team genuinely wants to be part of. And I want you to remember that your worth isn't measured by turnover numbers or satisfaction scores any more than theirs is.

And for all of you, I want you to know that what you do matters, not because someone told you it does, but because you feel it.

That's what this book is for."

Kat Nisson, MLIS, CPCC, brings expertise in leadership development, career coaching for those navigating workplace trauma, and building thriving team communities. She's also known for creating scripts and guidelines that build in excellence without sacrificing humanity and flexibility, proving that high standards and authentic connection aren't mutually exclusive.

Kat writes: "*The first time I successfully walked someone through a truly impossible guest situation, I realized the magic wasn't in what I said. It was in how I showed up. That moment shaped everything that came after.*

I've spent my career helping leaders navigate workplace trauma, build genuine community on teams, and prove that you can have both exacting standards and humanity. All of them are searching for the same thing: how to build cultures where people show up as their best selves, not their most exhausted selves.

I've seen what happens when teams operate from fear and what happens when they operate from worth. And I've learned that the organizations that get this right understand what Randy has been teaching for decades: authentic worth creates authentic service, and that's what creates magic."

Together, we wrote this book for the people who make hospitality work, and for the leaders who want to make it sustainable. If you're working on this where you are, we'd love to hear how it's going. The work continues at worthatwork.com, where you'll find conversations, resources, and ways to bring this into your own teams.